IN PURSUIT FOR
FREEDOM

LEVEE KADENGE

authorHOUSE®

AuthorHouse™
1663 Liberty Drive
Bloomington, IN 47403
www.authorhouse.com
Phone: 1 (800) 839-8640

Published by AuthorHouse 08/20/2018

ISBN: 978-1-5462-5669-4 (sc)
ISBN: 978-1-5462-5667-0 (hc)
ISBN: 978-1-5462-5668-7 (e)

Library of Congress Control Number: 2018909912

CONTENTS

PREFACE

Levee Kadenge was born in Kwenda and brought up by his parents. He is a product of a polygamous family. He narrates his childhood story that reveals rebellious aspects. As a young boy he experienced the youthful struggles of identity. As a result, this book has been written from real life situation. The material is drawn from the personal encounters of the author. His behaviours reveal the challenges of growing up. Like Moses in the bible Levee has a past and future that cannot converge. His past and future cannot build a connected history. It reveals the notorious life of a rural adolescent African boy, Levee, who upon completing his O' level studies could not find meaning in all that was around him. But later he champions the fight for good governance in church and government.

As he progresses in life he draws much from his father and mother. His father's response to the woman who insulted him and stripped herself naked in anger, when her maize field was destroyed by their bullock helps him to humbly respond, years later, to a woman who tore his bible at a church meeting in anger. Her mother's tears and prayers for him caused him to turn to God and build his faith. Levee's context and childhood experiences weave his courageous interaction with various people. His encounters with VaMukaka, who later helped in their fields give a context for his need to fight for the lives of other people in a nonviolent way.

This book is the result of a deep concern for human freedom and the cost of political engagement. Levee Kadenge is interested in the freedom of his people. Addressing the concerns of people of Zimbabwe, levee finds himself in trouble with the state agencies and his church decided to part ways with him. For it emerged that the Church, through Levee's activities with Christian Alliance, was accused of involving herself in the politics of the day. In a way the church in Africa has been a threat when it comes to matters of human rights. As a result, every time towards elections, the church has become a victim of abuse and torture.

Despite being aware of the cost of standing for a just society, Levee sacrifices his life and has been arrested several times for what he stood for. Various organisations were formed because of his courage to stand for freedom. He believes that peace, justice, forgiveness, and reconciliation come at a cost. He further accepts as true that the church which stands for God's love must advocate for the freedom of God's people. But alas, the church has shown cowardice around facing the evils committed by the politicians.

The love that he received from people of his colour and those of other nations humbles him. His book warns the reader to stand for justice and not to idolize anything at the expense of human dignity. He thus says;

- If we idolize anger and hate, we devalue healing and transformation.

- If we idolize violence we devalue life

- if we idolize wealth we create poverty

He encourages us to forgive but not to forget, for he believes that forgetting is sickness. He has forgiven the politicians, church members and its leadership. Nevertheless, he challenges the church not to be quiet when people are suffering for he strongly believes that, Evil thrives when good people are silent. For him Christianity without the Cross is costless and devoid of purpose.

Rev Dr Ananias K. Nyanjaya

PROLOGUE

The lesson you presented on 'The Role of the Minister in a Wesleyan Tradition' was very original, live and full of experiences. As a Methodist minister, you brought another dimension which made the session very lively. It was a memorable presentation indeed. We have benefited a lot from your personal experiences in the Methodist tradition. Life is not length of it, but its depth. You clearly demonstrated this. (1)

I received the above letter after I made a presentation on 7 January 2012 to Methodist ministers gathered at Pakame High School. After I received it I was convinced that it was time I write my memoirs. It all started with my colleague Rev Dr Jimmy Dube who gave me some hints on what to present on the topic. The following morning, he had changed his mind. He came to me and said "Old man, go and tell them your story. You have been in ministry for more than thirty years. Just share your experiences."

I immediately stopped researching and jotted some notes down about my experiences and hit the road to make my presentation. But the responses I got after the presentation were very encouraging. I vowed to put pen to paper and elaborate on my one-hour presentation in the form of a book. The work below is the result of the encouragement I got from many quarters including the presiding bishop himself.

(1) An extract from the Presiding Bishop of Methodist Church in Zimbabwe (MCZ), Rev Amos Ndhlumbi (23 February 2012)

INTRODUCTION

THE PURPOSE OF THIS BOOK

First and foremost, I want to thank the almighty God, the creator of the human mind, body and language, for giving me this rare opportunity to sit down and write a book about myself. In this book, I critically and meditatively reflect on my life. I go through all the major struggles that I have encountered and those that I deliberately involved myself in sharing my, in life. In it I also expresses my philosophical outlook. The book is not just about my achievements, but it also chronicles my struggles. Therefore, the questions that I am grappling with here are concerned with what I have done which has saved human lives and what I ought to do to save people.

As human beings we are always waging struggles against all sorts of adversaries. There are forces, whether physical or nonphysical, that are always working against us. For instance, some people are talented or are endowed with both the intellectual and physical powers to protect others and the environment from these forces. I strongly believe that I am one of them. My point of departure is that I maintain that issues such as politics, the environment, poverty, sexuality and in human life. Failure to recognize and respect these issues is a religious failure, to say the least.

This book critically examines my participation in the long and highly protracted struggle for democratic space in Zimbabwe. It also expresses my concern over the silence of some of my friends. The major question I am asking is: Why are the religious leaders quiet when things are getting wayward like this? Where is the voice of the Christians when inflation is above 8 000% and unemployment levels are well above 85%?

I am airing my views concerning the general Zimbabwean situation which is suffering because of a punctured economy.

In Zimbabwe today, there is no democracy both at government level and even in the Church. Therefore, I here in call for change in all established institutions in Zimbabwe. Why are things the way they are right now? Is it by God's design or its nature taking its course? Through this book I suggest solutions from a theologian's perspective. For these and others questions I try to provide solutions that have religious inclinations.

My massage is hinged on my understanding of theology. I strongly believe that theological discourse has the power to liberate the people's minds and souls. Theology can now critically challenge and at times physically and spiritually engage with some undemocratic systems. This is what I refer to as the Theology of Engagement where I am interested in engaging people for the betterment of their lives. We all want to live lives that are better than our present status. We are always struggling to improve our lives in pursuit for freedom. It is unfortunate thoughts that some people are employed by some evil systems to torture, kill or maim the powerless.

Therefore, this book also aims at equipping the individual with the knowledge that God is for us all. My commitment to the struggle for the liberation of the oppressed, the down-trodden, the marginalized and the segregated is one of the ways through which I confess my faith in God who loves all and sundry. The role that I have been playing in seeking justice for the people, creates a fruitful debate and 'engagement' with students of theology, Church ministers, government officials and all those who are interested in Zimbabwean theology especially its prophetic political dimensions. I am one of those Christians that believe that Christ's followers must always respond to any form of a crisis.

It is important to note that when Pharaoh oppressed the Children of Israel, Moses did not bless him. He went directly to him and rebuked him when he said to him "Let my people go." In other words, he was telling him that "do not oppress my people, free them." Therefore, it is the duty of the prophets to stand for the voiceless and the oppressed. In the following section I briefly describe the events or life experiences that have played an instrumental role in shaping my world view.

CHAPTER ONE

BACKGROUND

My mother, the late Theresa Kadenge, was a simple house wife. She was a serious disciplinarian who managed her home with great love. I will always cherish her love for the rest of my life. She looked after her children and all other relatives in a manner that I have never seen before. This can partly be explained by her background as a staunch Methodist. She religiously followed the Biblical teaching of love. In other words, she had a sound understanding of the Biblical tools for surviving. In addition, my mother keenly followed the day to day activities of the Church which is located a few kilometres away from our home. The Church is located in the schoolyard of Warikandwa Primary School. I, like John Wesley strongly believe that I was socialized into Methodism through my mother. I will always cherish her motherly love.

THE DAY I WAS BAPTIZED

Few people expect a drama during a well-prepared occasion like a baptism. But my tale is different.

Mum, God bless her, for she is now at rest, wanted all her children baptized. When I was seven years old, she learnt from the congregation leader at Warikandwa that the Church minister would be coming the following Sunday. She told us that we were going to be baptized that day.

1

Not that we were new to church. But what I had seen so far, plus the stories that boys of my age concocted about white men, began to fill my mind. Each time the white minister came from Kwenda mission he baptized both children and adults, when it was the babies' turn and they were handed over to the minister, most of them kicked out, as if there was something strange about him and they did not like the experience. Mothers seemed to be more concerned about the minister than their own babies. I thought these parents just did not realize they were subjecting their children to a dangerous man.

Sometimes the babies cried uncontrollably, this confirmed our suspicions, shared during the long cold winter afternoons when we were sent to look for stray cattle. We sat behind the anthills instead, telling stories and singing the children's song: *Zuva zuva ndiye Ishe – Gute gute murombo – 'sun sun, you are the king – cloud cloud, you are the poor one.'* Clouds and sun seemed to be competing in a race and when the sun came out we felt good, convinced it was the singing that had done it. The singing and the stories went on until sunset. One strange thing we remembered about the white man was that his hands looked like pieces of red-hot iron and we thought that that was why this minister must be producing so much heat that it made the babies cry.

We were born at a time when you could believe anything about the white people. Some of the strange expectations of the settler community could look very funny to a child. I remember a day when most of the men from a nearby village came to help with threshing the rapoko crop. When a jeep came along the road they all stopped and all those who had hats on lifted them up. My father was amused and said, "Son you will understand when you grow up." If we had not done that the truck might have stopped, and we could have been beaten up because we did not show respect to Ngosi who is the district commissioner. We are supposed to do that to all white men."

Back to the baptism issue. Until my mother broke the news, I thought that I had been baptized as a baby and would not have to face this ordeal again. Little did she realize my fears. Suddenly it was Sunday morning. We started getting ready to walk the mile to Church when we heard the minister's motorbike pass by our home.

My heart began to throb heavily. My brother set off to the well with water tins. I set off in the opposite direction and was some distance away before my mum called "where is Levee?" One of my brothers immediately spotted and said, "there he is!" This made me run further.

Mum sent all the boys (Christopher and Joshua, both my elder brothers) to catch me and the dog followed as well. I was its best friend and it just galloped up to me and waited for a game. But I kept on running thinking that if I go far enough away it would be too late for the Church service and I would be spared the hot iron man.

Little did I know that I was fooling myself. My elder brothers soon caught me and thumped me. Knowing that the Church service had started, they took me straight to Church, just as I was in my abnormally long shirt and not another stitch. For special days we had trousers and it was my fault I had not them on.

My mother was waiting patiently at the Church door. I was placed firmly in her loving hands and led quickly to the altar to join the queue of those who were to be baptized. As the minister came nearer to me I became so tense such that mum held me tight for I was very stiff. I was certain of only one thing that the heat of his hand would cook my head. To my utter surprise the hand was cool. The water that was streaming down my face felt so good. Surely, something changed me when I was baptized.

My Call

This reflection on my life and on Zimbabwean politics in general spans over a period of 40 years, that is, from 1977 to 2017, the period I was in active Methodist itinerant ministry having been accepted as a candidate for the ministry in 1977 and was sent to theological college the following year at United Theological College UTC in Epworth after13km to the east of the then Salisbury.

I strongly believe that I have now discovered my purpose in life at the right time. God created me for a purpose and it is this purpose that I have been vigorously trying to fulfil for the past 40 years. In my view, this is not a short period of time. This is primarily because this is the period during which I had direct contact and severe confrontation with the realities of life. This period has also witnessed a lot of things that have helped me make friends and create enemies. I know that I have created enemies and friends at home and abroad. These people come from diverse career histories and cultural backgrounds. Some of them have encouraged me while others have been busy trying to destroy me. Those who try to destroy my vision failed because mine was clear and purpose driven. These people do not know the nature of the divine powers that I am wielding. As such if asked to describe myself choosing between being a liberal, reformist, conservative or radical, I would without hesitation say that I am a "radical", who is pursuing freedom.

Interestingly, some of the people that I thought were my best friends have actually turned out to be my worst enemies. I will never hate them though. Instead, I love them and even pray for them. I will always constructively engage them so that one day they will realize that they have been totally lost.

I also want to stress the fact that there is nothing unique about this because some of my friends who are involved in prophetic work have told me similar stories. Even the prophets of the Biblical times had similar backgrounds. In this regard, they were not liked nor where they favoured by the ruling elite because they rebuked them.

Jesus also faced almost similar earthly challenges. Therefore, let it be known here and abroad that I will always speak against injustice as and when it is appropriate. One of the duties of earthly prophets is to rebuke earthly leaders whose ways of ruling are not consistent with the basic instructions that are unequivocally outlined in holy Word of God. We as prophets will always provide the checks and balances that will ensure earthly justice so that the Kingdom of God may come.

It is during the prolonged period of civil unrest and gross uncertainties for the generality of Zimbabweans that some of us have been labelled enemies of the state. Some people have called us cowards while others have defined us as traitors or members CIA. For example, one former Minister of Foreign Affairs in the Zimbabwe Nathan Shamuyarira, was one of those people who thought that I was a member of the CIA. I did not know why he thought that way. I was convinced that he wanted to please the President by labelling some of us all sorts of names.

Through this book I will try to interpret all these accusations and set the record straight. Before I do that, I want to stress the point that I do not mind all these accusations. I expect them because they are coming from people who hate truth tellers and people who do not understand or are afraid of prophetic politics.

Some Zimbabwean politicians claim to be Christians, but the truth of the matter is that they do not demonstrate or adhere to Christian values in their everyday activities. If one is truly a Christian, then why does he/she support an oppressive regime? Although it is not my duty to measure people's level of spirituality I cannot keep quiet when some people masquerade as Christians through the misuse of biblical verses. There are some who come to Church to buy votes. We know that and will always tell them that they are looking for the wrong things in God's House. Here I am referring to politicians who claim to be Christians but are oppressing the poor at the same time. Such kinds of people just want to manipulate the Church for their self-gain or unbridled quest for self-aggrandizement. They forget that God said that "Blessed are the poor in spirit for theirs is the kingdom of heaven." Matthew 5:3 KJV. The, truth is that some politicians do not fear God. It is not my duty to judge other people, but I will not hesitate to point out what they do that which is not Godly or consistent with Christian principles.

Why 40 years? These years are important in my life because they reflect and chronicle my life both during the pre-independence and the post-independence periods. In addition, this is the period when I have been actively involved and heavily grappling with crucial national issues both at home and abroad. Furthermore, this period is significant, at least for me, because the Church is celebrating 40 years of service as an autonomous Church. The theme of this celebration is "We know that everything God works for good with those who love him." Romans 8:28. It happens that this is one of the verses that are at the centre of my faith.

Growing up – Some light moments

The following are some of the stories that reflect my experiences. They are put here to just make this life history of mine real and down to earth. I remembered them one by one as I embarked on my story. They are not in order of occurrence but were some of the light moments in our eventful rural lives.

No 1. How *Skopu* died.

One bright day in my rural village we had assembled for a break at lunch. My father, Francis Kadenge, was keen to see that no one strayed because we had to go back to the fields. Little did father know that the undone was going to be done.

On this day, one of our troublesome cattle had done it again. This animal was fond of destroying our neighbours' gardens and mowing the vegetables in them. For a number of times this beast named *'skopu'* broke into one elderly lady, *Mbuya Chikonangombe's* treasured garden. On this day it had done it again.

As we had rested a bit, we suddenly heard a funny noise from behind our village. Anger knows no boundaries. The woman appeared exhausted and staggering. She spared no moment as she ran straight to our father who was sitting close to us. Within a flicker of a moment she lifted her dress bare in front of my father.

In local culture, this is the worst form through which a woman can show her disgust and anger. She cried saying, '*Yowe-e-ee*! you have killed me. Your cow has destroyed my garden again and now you deserve to see this', as she without undergarments inside revealed her private parts not only to my father but to all of us who were surprised that she could dare do such a thing in public. The woman did not want anyone to look into the issue. This was her way of saying enough is enough. As children we did not know how to behave but just to be mesmerised and wished this drama was over quickly. I am convinced the boys intently looked while the girls looked aside.

My father did not waste time. He quickly knelt before the woman and pleaded for mercy. I had never seen my father kneeling let alone to another woman. On this occasion he had no choice but to give in and ask for forgiveness. We as children looked at each other and wondered why father had not beaten her up. We later learnt that he could not have done that. He knew what it meant and was sorry for the incident.

Our day ended that way. We were spared going back to the fields. This happening made my father to think again about the cow which he had resisted to put away for a long time. We were instructed to go to fetch the cow right away. When we brought the animal father just instructed us to slaughter it. Before sunset we were enjoying the meat of *skopu*. Such was the end of our dear cow whose activities made us see what was not to be seen.

The local community was informed of the provision of meat for sale. The following day many locals came to buy meat from us. Some brought cash, others brought small grains like *rapoko* to exchange with a pound or two of meat. Before the end of the day *skopu* was finished. Father made sure that there was enough meat to take us for a while.

From this day on we had a story to share with friends at school. We learnt that it was common practise for local women to show their anger that way. The days that followed were of hard work. We had meat to eat and father made sure that we ate properly and worked much because we were being well fed. No one would dare miss a meal. So, for a while father did not trouble himself by making sure we did not elope. Nice afternoon meals gave us the impetus to work harder. Yes, we missed *skopu* but the meals we were now having compensated for the loss of a beloved animal.

Life in rural Zimbabwe is full of surprises. Dull moments are hard to come by. The woman whose garden was destroyed by *skopu* also bought meat for herself. Some few days later she remarked that she enjoyed eating *skopu* because it had grown fat because of her vegetables. However, peace returned to the community after the departure of *skopu*.

No.2, *Chigunwe (Toe)*

There was a man in our community who was always happy. This man had the misfortune of having lost all his toes except one. He only had his long toe left. He was thus nick-named *Chigunwe*, meaning 'Mr One Toe.' You could hear people say they saw *Chigunwe*, 'One Toe'. His case was obvious because he did not wear a pair of shoes on his feet.

One day there was a beer party at his home. Because of the popularity of this man people came from all corners of the community. Beer parties saved two main purposes. One was to socialise and the other was to provide for resources. Much of the beer would be sold so that the family would realise some cash to either send children to school or to buy food for the family.

The practice was that before each person bought a cup of beer he/she would be given *nzwisa*, a small cup for free to taste. It was quite a reasonable size.

Those with little hearts they would only need two cups to feel dizzy. This family was known of their generosity and their nzwisa was a little bigger.

As the day was going to a close and many had had too many cups of beer, there was a lot of singing and joy was on each and every visitor's face. From the looks of it the beer was good stuff and there was still plenty of it. There was enough to be sold for another day. Suddenly there were clouds and signs of rain were all over. As some patrons, were leaving some lightening, struck. The bolt was so powerful. This meant the bolt had struck within the village.

Smoke was immediately seen coming from the hut where *Chigunwe* had gone to rest. News was broken that *Chigunwe* had been struck by the bolt. People could not help but start mourning. There were sighs, of shock and there was pandemonium from all directions. Those who had covered some distance heard of the news and returned to the village.

For the next two days *Chigunwe*'s homestead became their temporary home. From the time *Chigunwe* died the beer was now for free. There was no need for people to go back home. The season was hot then and there was no need to fetch blankets. Beer became their blanket. For the great part of the evening there was so much noise which went into the middle of the night.

The following day a beast was slaughtered for meat for the mourners. Later when it was realised that there were too many people another beast was killed to feed the mourners. The send-off was so special because *Chigunwe* died when there was beer at his home. At our funerals beer would be sought for even from distant places. In the case of *Chigunwe* beer was already there. The beer which had been made for sale turned to free drink.

The story that went rounds was that *Chigunwe* died a befitting death. He was a good man and passed on when there was enough beer for all to share. It took several years to witness another memorable send off.

People in our village have always referred to *Chigunwe's* death because it was a death that matched his deeds. He died when all his friends were around. They honoured him by not going to their homes. They only left when they had buried their dear friend.

No 3, *VaMukaka* (*Mr Milkman*)

Friendship is real in rural Zimbabwe. There was this man who used to frequent our home. The man was never married. He carried no blanket but moved from village to village and was looked after by his hosts. He did not live long with any family. He stayed with those families that treated him well. When he felt he was no longer needed he would just bid farewell and hit the road for another home.

People liked him because he worked so hard. He was known as a man of the hoe. He would be very careful to avoid those things he felt his hosts would be worried about. In this case he would not always be right. One time he felt our family was bothered by his love for mukaka/milk. Upon his arrival on one of his visits he announced when he was a few yards from our homestead that he had stopped having milk.

My mother was not sure why he had announced that he was no longer interested in milk. Our visitor thought by declaring his disinterest in milk he would be more welcome. After some hard day's work my mother cooked sadza/traditional staple food which goes well with sour milk. Our visitor went ahead to eat milk more than before.

After taking milk he went on to explain that he had only declared his disinterest in milk because he had sensed that from the looks in people's faces he could only allay their fears by declaring that he was not going to eat milk. The reception he had received made him change his mind. The atmosphere had changed, and he felt comfortable to join in sharing food with any relish including milk.

From that time, he had mentioned his intention to stop taking milk he was given the name *VaMukaka*/milkman. The man lived a very long life. He was not the cleanest of people but would just wash to survive. Those who could afford to give him clothes did so to his pleasure. He would leave his other clothes for future use when he came back.

One thing about *VaMukaka* was that he was rarely ill. He worked hard. Many people thought because of his working hard he lived a long life. It was rare to see him disappointed. The fact that he managed to make several rounds in the neighbouring villages proved that he was a man of the people. Families would leave him looking after their homes if they wanted to visit. He would accept looking after one's home on condition that the neighbouring family would provide food. He hated cooking for himself.

That was when I learnt in life that one could spend the rest of one's life being looked after by well-wishers. Most of the people who looked after this man were not related to him. He was one with a difference. What he loved was his food and his work. He would always be quite waiting to be told what work to do by anyone any time. Such was a man who went about doing good. I do not remember seeing him angry. He wished everyone well and everyone wished him well. To some of us he was very innocent. No wonder people called him *munhu waMwari*/ man of God. He lived by example. In a sense he worked for his food. *VaMukaka* died at a very old age. He was remembered for hard work, friendship, caring and for eating well. I remember someone remarking that VaMukaka had good appetite. He ate anything anytime. He did not make life difficult for his hosts.

No, 4. *VaGonofiri kanguruve kadiki (Young pig)*

Close to our home lived a man who was very religious. His church did not allow him to eat pork. One day he came to our home. We kept pigs and we had slaughtered one. So, he asked us what kind of meat we were eating. We told him it was pork. He further asked us whether it was a big one or a small one, a piglet. His face glowed when we told him that it was very young. He then proceeded to eat.

When my father came and saw him eating, this man quickly defended what he was doing. He said to us his church forbade him from eating big pigs. Piglets were okay, and they did not call them pigs but gave them a name which he said was *gonofiri*. No one knew what that meant and from that day on he was called *vaGonofiri kanguruve kadiki*, meaning "Mr *Gonofiri*, the small pig."

No, 5. One tooth brush, one towel

In 1968, there were three of us who went to high school from my family. Our elder brother Joshua went to Tegwani/ (now Thekwani) Secondary school in Matebeleland in Southern Zimbabwe together with myself and the other brother Christopher went to St Marys Secondary School. St Marys is at the outskates of Harare in Chitungwiza. We had never put on shoes before. Our new school was one out of many. Shoes were compulsorily part of uniform. Actually, fees included a pair of shoes which we called mono-bond. Whatever that name meant but it was a tough shoe. We loved it. In our case this was a first shoe. We spent several days just not believing our luck.

Our father was indeed a genius. He went with us to introduce us to the school authorities. When he was talking to the boarding master he asked for a special favour. He pleaded with the boarding master to put the two of in one dormitory because we had one towel and one tooth brush. The man laughed but my father did not take that lightly. The authorities gave in and for the whole year we slept in one dormitory. Such was our first year in secondary school.

CHAPTER TWO

FAMILY BACKGROUND

I want to briefly share with the readers my family background that reveals the nature of the family that I come from, my childhood life and my status. I am not going to be very detailed/exhaustive, but I am just going to briefly outline those aspects of my life that are relevant to the focus of this book.

I was born in a polygamous family of two mothers and 14 children, 11 boys and three girls, among whom I am the fourth son. (Joshua, Christopher, Maxwell, myself, Lovemore, Clever, Phineas, Charles, Phanuel, Thomas, Raphael, Pricilla, Fortunate and Emily). My father, Mr Francis Kadenge was not formally employed. However, life was not very tough for him because he owned lots of cattle, sheep, pigs and goats. His wealth was enough to pay school fees for all his children. It was during the colonial era on the 4th of March 1953 at Chikanya Kraal in Chivhu district that I was born.

The Kadenge family is now established in the Magaisa or Mangisi village in Chikomba province, about 7km from Kwenda mission and almost 1km from Warikandwa school. My father, Mr Francis Kadenge, moved his family here because he could not find enough space for his two wives, Jane Chabvuta and the late Teresa Mukomba my mother. Our rural homestead is found 20km the North of Sadza Growth Point. The nearest schools to our rural home are Kwenda Secondary school and Warikandwa Primary and Secondary schools.

Life in rural and remote Njanja is very simple, magnanimously exciting, sometimes enjoyable and very peaceful. It is a "reserved area." In Shona we call it *'ruzevha'*. This Shona term was borrowed from the English word 'reserve'. It has been modified by Shona speakers to suite the pronunciation requirements of the Shona language.

It is common knowledge that the colonization of Zimbabwe and perhaps most African countries gave rise to an imbalanced sharing of land. However, since my father the late Francis Kadenge was a well-known Master Farmer and a very hard-working man we managed to make ends meet from tilling the land. He grew crops like potatoes, tomatoes, peas, carrots and beans for sale to local schools. He was a successful peasant farmer. He produced much more than what the newly resettled A2 and A1 farmers could produce today. He was awarded his Master Farmer's certificate in 1964 and was subsequently offered a farm by the Rhodesian Government in Gokwe but he preferred not to relocate because he wanted us to go to school. There were no schools in the farms. Others who were also awarded similar certificates grabbed the offer but failed to educate their Children because they were not producing enough crops for sale so that they can raise money to pay school fees. The land was our sole source of livelihood.

It is from these harsh economic background, that I learnt that hard work yields success. I have worked very hard in my life and I will continue to do so if I have strength to do so. I worked hard both in the fields and in school. Because my father was a hardworking man he also expected all his children to work very hard. He had his own special principles of life. I remember vividly that he would always tell us that "If you work very hard, then you should eat very hard but no work no food." It was some kind of 'food for work' framework. Probably the government learnt about this policy from the sage philosophy of my father and his contemporaries. Even today I eat hard because I work hard.

The courageous spirit in me

In addition, besides the fact that my father was a hardworking peasant farmer he was also a courageous man. This is one of the virtues of life that I genetically inherited from him. There is an occasion that I will never forget in my life. However, this occasion demonstrated how brave I have always been since my childhood.

This story is very sad story, but I cannot afford not to say something about it because I have learnt a lot from it. In 1961 my elder brothers Joshua, Christopher, Maxwell and I went to herd cattle as usual in the nearby pasture. We decided to swim in a shallow stream which is just behind our homestead. Sadly, my brother Maxwell failed to swim and disappeared. Joshua and Christopher who are older than I did not have the courage to go and tell our mother that Maxwell could not come out of the water. Even though I knew very well that she was going to thoroughly beat us I ran straight home to inform our mother about the disappearance of Maxwell. Unfortunately, when our mother came to rescue him he was already dead. From then we were never allowed to swim. Right now, I cannot swim. To make matters worse all my brothers and sisters cannot swim and fish. What was unusual about my behaviour since childhood is that I was always quick to report or reveal all bizarre things or situations.

My theological convictions

As mentioned above this chapter articulates the nature of theology that I have learnt and practiced and will continue to practice, that is, the Theology of Engagement. The nature of theology that I do hinges on a critical analysis of the sanctity and ethic of human life. I believe that life is special and as such should be respected as much as possible. In other words, I believe that human life is sacrosanct. The Holy-Book of God uncompromisingly deplores a deliberate negligence of human upliftment. Therefore, my Christian massage has been consistent and has always emphasized that life is a special gift from God. I have always wanted to develop and pursue a kind of theology that makes meaningful and significant contributions to the religious, political, economic and social transformation of people: Theology of Engagement.

I also strongly believe that everything that was created by God is good for human survival. Each aspect of creation deserves art-most respect from the human species. This means that all the things that we do every day have a direct bearing on Human life. What makes human life much more important than any other form of creation is the fact that Man was created in the image of God. Therefore, who on earth has the right to eliminate God's image? Who on earth has a legitimate right to starve someone who is endowed with the image of God?

While my main aim is to see the lives of people being transformed I also want to clearly demonstrate how my life has been changing because of my experiences for the past 40 years. I have grown up accustomed to seeing power abused. I cannot keep quiet when power is being abused by the powers that be. I will always rebuke those who abuse power, and this is consistent with Biblical teachings. I have always tried to develop my sermons from my everyday experiences. This is the only way I can demonstrate my relevance in society. I preach the things that people eat, see and smell every day. Thus, I develop my sermons from observable phenomena.

Even as I practice my freelance journalism I write about things that people experience every day. This is how I perceive the world, and this is how I hope to transform people's lives.

I also think that people need empowerment for them to resist injustice. This empowerment usually takes the form of knowledge. This means that it is the duty of the technocrats to think about and interpret everyday events for the people. Therefore, I will always try by every means to empower the people with the required faith and ideas for them to resist oppression. I use my faith, knowledge and works to cultivate or to develop capacity in people.

At the end in 1977 I joined the staff of Kwenda Secondary School to teach English Language and Geography. Kwenda is located to the West and is 7 kilometres away from my original rural home. It is the nearest mission boarding school to my home area. This is one of the schools that brought enlightenment in the form of formal education in the Chikomba district. Although I had other duties at the school such as directing the Scripture Union I mainly concentrated on my teaching responsibilities. This is primarily because I enjoyed, and I still enjoy teaching. Most of my sermons have lots of teaching elements in them. Moreover, these are the subjects that I was good at when I was still in school. My Geography teacher was very good, and I will always admire his dedication to duty. He is one of the teachers that I will never forget in my life.

It was at the end of this same year, that is 1977, that I had an unforgettable encounter with the freedom fighters at Kwenda Mission. This was during the height of the liberation war of liberation. Most often, mission schools were targeted by both the colonial regimes soldiers and liberation army because this is where all the missionaries were located. The "comrades" who were operating in my home area also deliberately targeted this mission school because they wanted to wantonly loot our salaries and all sorts of belongings such as food, clothes and wrist watches.

I will never forget one occasion when the comrades came to organize a *pungwe* at Kwenda Mission. During the *pungwe* one of the comrades called me aside as if he had some serious issues to discuss with me. He asked me to give him my brand new, pair of jean trousers and my shirt. There was no way I could resist such kind of requests because that was risking my life. I just had to give him, and he gave me his tattered and dirty pair of trousers and T-shirt.

It is common knowledge in Zimbabwe that all sorts of unwarranted brutal atrocities were being committed by both the comrades and the soldiers. Some rural man and Woman were killed, and some were buried alive. All these are the likely consequences of a war. Normally a war is bloody. This is why I am always against violent confrontations. I directly experienced the detrimental consequences of war situations. They are too gustily to contemplate.

Some of the comrades (freedom fighters) who were operating around Kwenda Mission tried by every means to discourage me from joining the Christian ministry. They were totally against my idea of training as a pastor. Why? Their argument was very ridiculous. It totally reflected that some of them lacked knowledge of the crucial Biblical teachings. Their poor argument was that I should not go to a place where Jesus is taught because, at least according to them, "Jesus is not God but a son of Mary who was born out of wedlock." They emphasized that I should learn about God and not Jesus. Even up until now I do not understand how they understood the Bible. It is very unfortunate that some of the people who waged the war against colonial bondage did not know God. So, why were they fighting the liberation struggle?

I am one person who is unstoppable when it comes to educating myself. I actually felt like taking the comrades to Church because they needed a thorough Bible teaching. They needed a strong prayer so that they may know God. They also did not realize that it was God who was guiding them throughout the liberation struggle. Who on earth has the power to dislodge despondent leaders? It can only be God.

However, despite their discouragement I joined as a Theology student in 1978 at the height of the liberation struggle. This institution is run by seven denominations and students from these Churches train together. UTC is one of its kind and has demonstrated what ecclesiastical ecumenism should be. During my time there as a student we had some members from the African Initiated Churches training with us. During vacations I did not stop going back home even though it was dangerous until the country got its independence from Britain in 1980. It is from such an experience that I reflect on my life focusing on the past 40 years. This experience is my primary source of inspiration.

The Church and National Development: Reminiscing on the Past Experiences

I have always maintained the idea that the Church has a role to play on issues relating to national development. National development involves the rate at which people have access to human needs. It measures our access to important developmental skills such as vocational training and formal education. I have always been an advocate for projects and programmes that enhance productivity, social and economic growth. This can only be achieved when Zimbabwean Church ministers play their part as far as prophetic action is concerned in the Zimbabwean context. We should play our priestly roles while at the same time advocating for peaceful coexistence. These are some of the fundamental principles that we should always keep in mind every time we execute our duties as Christian leaders.

When I was ministering in the Matabeleland region I advocated the participation of the Church in activities that bring about national development. Here is a paper that I presented at the Methodist Church in Zimbabwe Bulawayo Synod in 1984, tackling the question of the role of the Church in national development. The paper is entitled "A Response to ZCC paper on Churches' Commitment to Development."

"Development is seen succeeding in a situation where there is meaningful distribution of wealth. Technology needs to be developed but not at the peril of the masses- e.g. the computer deprives many workers from being employed simply because the computer can do the work of such a number of people.

We need our own identity, that is, a product of the past and the present-hence the production of the 'Zimbabwean Society'.

Our Church is involved in development. The leaders saw the need and worked with the people to see exactly what the areas of immediate need were. Two young men will be sent from Binga to go and train in Elementary Agriculture so that they go back to their people and show, by example, some better methods of farming. We seek development funds so that our proposed projects may get off the ground.

The Church is prepared to listen to God who speaks even through men and through different situations. But the Church needs its basic independence – that is, to be able to see facts as they are and either hail them or criticize them, as the case may be. We, therefore, cannot be non-political, yet this does not mean that the Churches should engage in petty-party politics. Individuals can join political parties of their choice, but this should not be interpreted as Church involvement in politics. The Church is a unifying factor and should always preach reconciliation between politicians and other Christians as well.

The poor still have unanswered questions, despite their appreciation for what the Church is doing to help them. These questions will, however, be answered as the Church continues to focus on the Spirit of God and seek direction from God and from God alone.

The Gospel demands that people should repent and be saved. The Church is prepared to identify with the oppressed and the poor.

Development cannot necessarily be Evangelism because not all those involved in development are involved in what the Church knows as Evangelism. Humanitarian services are not equated with Evangelism.

The government is involved in many projects. So far, the Church sees no particular area of real conflict but is prepared to warn the Government on any area that it sees is in conflict with development.

We need to focus our attention on God through Jesus Christ and by the inspiration of the Holy Spirit, move into the future in <u>Faith</u>."

The short paper that has been given above surely outlines the role of the Church in developing the nation. I have always upheld the view that the Church should stand and support the oppressed and the poor. Even in the 1980s, I was very conscious of the struggle of the oppressed and marginalized people of Zimbabwe. The Church should be seen to be working flat-out for the total emancipation and socio-economic transformation and development of the poor. As echoed in the paper it is the purpose of the Church to seek ways and methods for conflict resolution. This is the philosophy that guides the theological and political reflections that I am doing these days. I will not hesitate to warn the politicians whenever their actions infringe the rights of the people. Gone are the days when the Churches were far from being at odds with oppressive systems. I still maintain that the Church has a crucial, strong and positive role to play in national development. The Church must act as a prophetic voice. It must be a voice of the voiceless.

CHAPTER THREE

THE RADICAL LEVEE

The land mark in my life was in 1972 at the New celebrations at our local Church as was the practise on our, "circuit." Our local church at Warikandwa always celebrated new year in style. This was the practise in our circuit. Societies were required to congregate the whole night to wait for the new year eve. Under normal circumstances people left the church early in the morning on the 1st January. These celebrations were attended by many people from the local villages. It is also interesting to note that the majority of people from my original home area are Methodists.

Strangely before we attended the Church service we drank some rural traditional beer which is popularly known as 'Seven Days'. It is referred to as Seven Days because it takes seven days to ferment before people can drink it. In Zimbabwe this is the type of beer that is used for most African traditional ceremonies such as Kurova guva and Bira. They were four of us who had just finished Form 4. The community looked to us as very educated youngsters with bright future. We would have walked more than 20km in search for the right staff. The community never quite understood why we behaved like that. Our parents had nearly given up let alone my mother, who always had early morning prayers for us.

Around 4am in the morning she would wake up praying loudly from her room. She would pray like *"Mwari ivaiwo nemwanakomana wangu Levee. Ko chii chandakatadza kuti aite zvaari kuita. Kana chiripo ndiregerereiwo."* (Lord be with my son Levee. What did I do wrong that has made him behave this way? If there is anything wrong I did please forgive me.) She would say that on a daily basis. I would wake up my siblings and started laughing at her prayer.

By the time we got to Church around 11.30pm we were very drunk. I will never forget this fateful day because on this day my friends and I embarrassed our families because we brought beer in the Church. I had a calabash of beer rapped in a large jacked that we picked from home. The church was full, but the front bench had just enough space for the 4 of us. We went straight for the empty seats. I was still clinging to my calabash. We started fidgeting around causing lots of noise while the preacher was delivering a sermon in preparation for 12 the midnight celebration. Twelve midnight was the climax. People would shout and make much noise in praise and worship and then calm for more celebrations until dawn.

Meantime the calabash slipped through the jacket and rolled towards the preacher. When those in front saw this people started screaming and there was pandemonium. The four of us rose up and started singing *"Muka Jonah tinamate..."* (rise Jonah and let us pray....) It was a popular Christian song. In that confusion church members left the church confused. We went out and started throwing stones on the corrugated roof of the church. People ran for their lives. Midnight was just few minutes away, but worshippers had left fearing for their lives. The preacher man did not have time to officially send people away. Everyone left, and the church was deserted. This was the first of its kind. The whole community was puzzled and did not understand why such an educated group of young people could just do that. I left for home now pondering what to do. Now I was on my own, my friends had deserted me. I was the oldest among the group.

Flight to Harare

The following morning after the church saga, I left home by bus without telling anyone. Somehow, I am convinced I told my mother. By afternoon

I was in Harare about 160km away, I did not stay long that same evening I left for Mhondoro, my mother's birth place, some 78km away from Harare. My mother's home by this time was in Watyoka village. They came from Marumha village across Mupfure river. Marumha is closer to the Mission, Sandrigham/Chivero. My mother went to Gonza school when it was known as Marumha before the change. These places are all in Mhondoro.

My uncle made sure there was beer every day in their home. Because of this demand they had to resort to brewing what they called chiwhani/ (one day brew), meaning that beer made from lots of yeast and sugar. It is made in the evening and the following day it is served and knocks people off. Coming from a beer starved situation in my home area I was now staying in a home where it was never dry. I just drained myself in beer from the day I arrived. I ate very little and drank so much beer. So, from 2nd to 11th January 1973 I was never dry as, it was. I just do not know how I made it.

On 11th I had to go back to Harare to stay with my cousin brother Evenness Zvomuya in Highfield high density area in Canaan section. My cousin did not drink beer. Though he was very anti beer he did not chase me away from his place. Up to now I do not know how I arrived at his home. He only told me that I arrived dead drunk and not able to talk. The following morning a lady friend of his came and invited me to church which was just a few metres away. It was an Apostolic Faith Mission (AFM). There was a whole week crusade being led by a very powerful Evangelist by the name Mr Kupara.

Initially I said to her, no. After a little persuasion I agreed. So, the three of us left for the service around 7pm. Evangelist Kupara delivered a fiery sermon. I was very impressed but just said to myself it's good stuff for women. Sooner had he called worshippers to alter and not to my surprise the bulk of the people who went there were women. He prayed for all of them and he was sweating at the end. He made a second call and fewer numbers went. After he made the third and what he called final call I decide to go just for fun. My cousin could not believe what he was witnessing. He thought I was going to cause trouble.

Now there were very few of us, if not three only. He had enough time for each one of us. When it came to my turn he just asked, "What can I pray for young man?" The answer was very simple, "All the bad you preached that people do, I do." He laid his hands on my head and prayed like he never prayed before. I really felt something was happening in me but could not make sense of it. On our way home, my brother just dismissed my promises that I was going to stop smoking and drinking. He had had enough of those empty promises. I was adamant, though, that I would finish my cigar stub I had left at home. Indeed, I sat down, lit the cigar and enjoyed it. And that was the last of my smoking and drinking habits.

I never went back to AFM. My distant cousin who was Evenness' cousin brother Charles Chihota who was my age mate took me in and I joined him going to his church Roman Catholic in Lusaka section of Highfield township. My desire to serve God was growing. I decided to join Catholic brotherhood. As I was lying on bed in the afternoon one day, I had a vision in which lots of terrifying creatures came for me. Immediately when I woke up I shouted, 'no, no, I am not going to join celibacy ministry.' I took this to mean coming problems. I never went back to Catholic church.

Now I was on a hunt for my church of baptism. I looked for the Methodist church which was close by. Before I had asked about the procedure to enter ministry I found myself at UTC. I had inquired about its where about. I walked 48km to and back. The principal a white man Rev Peter Russell, a Methodist told me to go back to my church and be told how one candidates for ministry. Little did I know that it was going to take me five years before I was to be admitted at UTC.

My Candidature: Child of 'sin'

My candidature was not easy. On the day the church had to vote for me for admission as a candidature there was real drama at that meeting as was the practice, I was asked to leave the meeting so that members of the meeting could be free to discuss the candidate and then vote for or against the forwarding of the name. One Evangelist who claimed to know me better than others stood to give his views on my candidature. He told the meeting that it was not proper for the church to accept someone who was a product of sin. Being born from the second wife in a polygamous marriage meant, according to him that my mother was not married by Christian custom hence that should disqualify me from entering ministry. The debate took long, and I was wondering what was happening as I remained for quite some time outside.

Finally, a vote had to be taken. The meeting unanimously agreed that I should proceed in spite of the 'vital' information shared by the evangelist. I just wondered if those many in the ministry who do not even know their fathers would be treated. Worse if one was a product of rape etc. Such was the thinking of some men and women of God. I forgave the man. He did not know what he was doing. But he thought he was protecting the church. He, however, was not very far from the church's teaching then.

Insurance Salesman, Teacher and Local Preacher

When I finally resolved to enter ministry, I left Harare, after I had had a stint on insurance salesmanship. I really enjoyed selling insurance policies throughout the country. We were trained by a Mr Chikanya of the Insurance Co-operation of Rhodesia (ICR). I quickly mastered the art of selling insurance and hit the road selling insurance to teachers and all and sundry who dared listen to this new convert both of Christianity and of the insurance industry. A number of my clients accepted both Christ and insurance policies. If one did not take one, they went for the other.

However, my call to ministry was being compromised by travelling. It was recommended that I settle in one place so that I could begin the process of becoming a full Local Preacher. One had to train as a Local Preacher first before he/she could be processed into candidature. The only place I could do it comfortably was going back home. My family welcomed me back with great joy. The principal of Kwenda Secondary school, Rev Ed Standhaft invited me to teach in the primary school because both the Secondary and Primary came under his Superintendence. I taught for a very short period and then was transferred to Sengwe primary school 60km away for just a term and came back to secondary school where I was teaching English, Geography and Religious studies.

Meantime I was being processed as a Local Preacher. After two years I was fully accredited preacher and immediately my candidature process started. I was supposed to enter College in 1977 but I was not accepted by the Candidates Committee. The reason was that I had read too many charismatic books (76) of them in two years. It was recommended that I should read other books which could make me a balanced Christian and not a charismatic fundamentalist which I had become. Mr John Mellor and Mrs Mellor who replaced Rev Standhaft were Methodists but on the charismatic side. They had many of these charismatic books which I read like a hungry lion. I began my ministerial studies at UTC, in 1978.

Educational Background

I went to school at a fairly young age. I did my primary education at Warikandwa Primary school. There was no secondary school close to our village. Those who had supportive parents were sent to boarding schools, usually Church schools to further their education. My appetite for knowledge has always been insatiable. In 1968 I enrolled for my Secondary education at St. Mary's an Anglican school (Hunyani). I wrote my O Levels in 1971. Thereafter, in 1978 I enrolled for a Diploma in Theological Studies at the United Theological College in Harare, Zimbabwe. This was my first tertiary academic qualification. It created the foundation or platform upon which all the other educational successes came about. I studied for my first degree through correspondence with UNISA University of South Africa UNISA from 1980 to 1983. I graduated with my Bachelor of Theology degree in 1983. I was very happy to be one of the graduates to hail from my remote Chikomba province. I was the first university graduate from my village and I was also the first university graduate in my family. This made us proud as a whole family. However, some of my younger brothers learnt a lesson from me and today most of them are graduates in various academic areas. I composed a little prayer soon after graduation and it reads,

> *"Thank God I started studying for the Bachelor of Theology Degree in 1980 and finished in 1982. Though it was a strenuous exercise I did however enjoy the hard-worn Degree. This initial Degree must have many more to come. Thank God he has given me the power to read and study fruitfully."*

Surely "many more" degrees came. This small prayer clearly shows how faithful I have always been to my ever-powerful God. Soon after successfully completing of my first Degree I got a scholarship to pursue a postgraduate Diploma in Theology at the University of Bristol (UK) from 1984 to 1985. In partial fulfilment of the requirements of the Diploma in Theology I submitted a dissertation entitled "A Study of the Relationship between Missionary Activity and the Growth of African Nationalism in Zimbabwe." In this dissertation, I examined in detail the role of the missionary activities in colonizing Zimbabwe, in education and the impact of missionary activities in Zimbabwean land usage. It was not easy to write a thesis on such aspects of Zimbabwean history because it was just after Zimbabwean's war of liberation. To make matters worse I was doing it in the British territory. Some academics were not happy with the way I presented my arguments because they accused me of being too Afrocentric. However, I stood my ground, managed to defend the arguments, that I vehemently proffered in this dissertation.

CHAPTER FOUR

WHY WRITE MEMOIRS NOW

I have always desired to write my memoirs since 2007. I did make some moves by writing some drafts which I put aside for no apparent reason. As recounted elsewhere before it was in January 2012 that I was invited by the Presiding Bishop Rev Amos Ndhlumbi to present a paper on "THE ROLE OF A MINISTER IN A WESLEYAN TRADITION" to Methodist Church in Zimbabwe ministers' Leadership seminar held at Pakame High School from 5 - 8 January 2012. As I was preparing for the paper by researching in the Library I called my colleague the Rev Dr Jimmy Dube for more ideas on the topic. He jotted down some good ideas. The following morning, he came to my house and he had changed his mind. He just said, "Old man, go and tell them your story. You have been in ministry for more than thirty years. Just share your experiences." I took heed and just went like I was with facts in my head. The response from the clergy after my presentation and the subsequent letter for the bishop appreciating what I did propelled me to revisit my notes for my memoirs.

The Presentation

John and Charles Wesley's ministry arose because of a 'context and a crisis' that prevailed both in England and the Church of England in the 18th century. The Church was no longer serving its purpose of ministering the people. England was going through a serious social crisis in the 1700 that led people to live rough, eat rough and drink rough. It was a dog eat dog situation. The church was not there to help the situation. The two brothers and colleagues came to rescue the situation. They did an excellent job of challenging the church not by just talking but by taking a position through organising people for the task of changing the situation by preaching to people to repent and move from their deplorable conditions to better life. Had it not been of the Wesleyans England could have sunk into abyss. Their work was at a cost and this did not affect their resolve. Instead they moved from strength to strength.

The Wesleyan brothers were not trained to do what they did. They were educated to read the context and crisis and to respond accordingly. Contexts and crisis differ from time to time and from situation to situation. So, there is no blue print as to how to respond. What is important are the tools of reading and responding to situations which we all got when we went for training. We trained to read the context and respond accordingly.

A pastor helps others to see clearly. Coming nearer home the first leader of ANC was a minister, Rev John Dube and his Chaplain was also a Wesleyan minister Rev Mqoboli Mahabane in 1923. The first leader of a political party in Southern Rhodesia was a Wesleyan minister Rev T.D Samkange in 1947. Bishop Abel T. Muzorewa another Wesleyan minister was the first black Prime Minister in Zimbabwe-Rhodesia in 1979. At the time the country was called Zimbabwe -Rhodesia, just to appease the whites, Bishop Muzorewa thus became the midwife of our independence in 1980. No wonder Professor Canaan Banana became the first president of Independent Zimbabwe in 1980. The Rev Matthew Rusike read his own context and the crisis of homelessness and started a Children's home in his own home in the sixties.

My presentation on that day was to share with them the role of a minister, myself who had travelled 34 years in a Wesleyan tradition. This is just one story; there are many stories that can be told by all of you gathered here today.

Life in College

Coming to United Theological College (UTC) in 1978 was yet another experience which marked the beginning of so many other things to come. I had left formal education in 1971. Theological education was not only new to me but was also very confusing to the extent that the first term I failed all the subjects. My lecturers did not give up. It seems all were encouraging me. The end of year results showed that I had passed all the subjects at last. My confidence returned. Two years later I could proceed to register with UNISA for a Bachelor of Theology Degree which I then finished in 1983 while I was at Ndolwane in Plumtree.

I have always wanted to be myself and that did not always endear well with others in College. One day as was the normal practise on Wednesdays, I went to College Chapel for the early morning service which normally ended with receiving Holy Communion. To my shock, the lecturer who was presiding over the Communion, the late Rev Jonah Kawadza had no clerical shirt on. He was dressed in a shirt with a tie and a gown. This was my first time to experience such, so I boycotted the Communion. I later protested to him that he was dressed improperly for the occasion. His explanation was very clear. He said that it did not matter very much and after all there were various denominations represented on compass and they did not put the same emphasis on ministerial attire. At least I got educated that day, but unfortunately, I had missed my communion that day because I thought my view on clerical attire was the only one correct.

After two years in College, my classmate from the same church Rev Claudius Matsikiti and I were called by the Principal, the Rev Dr CCG Mazobere, who was also from our church. While we were in his house he broke good and bad news to us. The good news was for my colleague and bad news was for me. "You Levee you are a bad guy and you will not be given the opportunity to study with University of South Africa (UNISA). *Iwe* (you) Claudius you have proved to be a very co-operative student, so you must go to the Church's Head Office and pick your forms for application to study with UNISA so that you start studies forthwith," he said.

The University of South Africa was, and still is, one of the best Distance educational institution in the world. I was left dumbfounded. I knew why. The politics at the College was such that if you did not belong to the same political party with the Principal, then you would pay heavily for that for, the college was divided into two groups, those who supported Zimbabwe African Peoples' party Patriotic Party (ZAPU-PF) and those who supported Zimbabwe African National Union, Patriotic Front (ZANU-PF). I happened to be supporting ZANU-PF and was not apologetic about that. I actually voted for Robert Mugabe in 1980, and this was my pay-back. My colleague would be taken by night to the other party's meetings by the Principal and this was not a secret.

So that year my colleague embarked on the UNISA programme. The Principal was, in the meantime, designated to head our church as President of Conference and I thought all hell had broken loose on me. He was going to lead the Methodist Church in the following year. Then the Principal moved to head the church. Meantime the new Principal, Rev Litsietsi Dube (now Bishop Dube) of the Evangelical Lutheran Church ELCZ, approached me and asked me why I was not studying with UNISA like my colleague. He then offered to look for a scholarship for me from his church. He promised that there were no strings attached. I would be given a scholarship by the ELCZ as a student of UTC and would proceed to work for my church. That was the best news I had ever had at UTC. The problem then was how would my church take it since the head of our church was the one who had stopped me.

However, the new principal approached the MCZ Head Office and Mr Kenneth Worger, the then Administrator of the Church also expressed concern, but he thought it was college policy that only one student from the church would be allowed to proceed for further studies. Meantime the Head of the church was out of the country and Mr Kenneth Worger was going to consult with him when he was back. Rev Dube assured the administrator that the ELCZ was prepared to fund my studies with UNISA. Before Mr Worger consulted the Head of the Church on his return, there were some very nasty developments which forced the President of the Church to be relieved of his post as leader of the church. As students we were not privy of what was happening in the church. We only heard, some days later, that we had an Acting President for the church. Mr Worger went ahead to process my registration with UNISA to be paid for by my church. Thus, the ELCZ was spared the burden to pay for my fees. To this day I remain grateful to retired Bishop Dube for such a gesture.

As if that was not enough, Rev Dube decided for all the students who had embarked on UNISA studies to go for an orientation at UNISA in Pretoria. For most of us this was our first trip outside Zimbabwe. Passports were organised quickly, and the trip was fully sponsored by the College. We were the twelve of us who made our maiden journey to SA and we were well looked after by Lutheran Church Members in both Mamelody and Altredgevile black townships in Pretoria. Local Lutheran pastors had asked members of their congregations to volunteer to look after us for two weeks. I stayed with a very well to do family who were not concerned about the struggle. They were so well-off enough that freedom fighters were really a bother to them. They had everything they wanted. They had a double storey house and a number of maids. Such was the disparity in SA. For those days I was with them I made sure that I did not talk any politics.

The experiences at UNISA main campus were an eye opener. By then we the blacks could not use the same buses with whites. Toilets were separate. Africans used their own, while whites did the same but at the same campus. I also saw benches labelled for blacks and whites separately.

The lecturers, who most of them were white Afrikaners were the most liberal I have ever met. I remember the seven of us sitting in one lecturer's office, some on tables and some on the floor and he seemed to have enjoyed that spectacle. We wished if we could have stayed longer. The result of our visit was that our determination to study was enhanced and I was determined to finish in three years which I did. Such was the inspiration that we got from our encounter with our various lecturers.

CHAPTER FIVE

PIONEERS OF KUSHINGA-PHIKELELA

Kushinga-Phikelela is a Technical College which is 20kn from Marondera. The double barrel name *Kushinga-Phikelela* comes from both Shona and Ndebele language which means perseverance, respectively. It started as an Agricultural College in 1981. It was the brain child of Professor Canaan Banana when he was President of the Republic Zimbabwe. He muted the idea in 1980 and invited volunteers from Chibero Africultural, United Theological College and the University of Zimbabwe. Together there were 7 students who heeded the call. Rev Allen Gurupira of United Methodist, who is currently the *Murewa* District Superintendent for *Murewa* District and myself represented UTC. Two others came from *Chibero* and three from UZ. This was during the 1980-81 vacation between December to January.

The College is built on a farm which was one of the first to be appropriated from white farmers. The farmer was given another farm somewhere else. There was a big farmhouse which became Administration Office. The seven of us stayed in the compound about one and half km away where workers lived. For the first week, we had no food. As students, we came with no money because we had been promised that we would be supplied with everything. The absence of food was an oversight on the part of the State House, we were later informed.

The president was told that food had been sent to us. For that week we survived on wild fruits called *mazhanje*. We would eat them throughout the day. We did the work of weeding by hoes which was supposed to be done by farm workers who had moved away with their previous employer. To our surprise no one of our group chickened out.

That was my first opportunity to do voluntary work almost two months. It was a relief when our provisions finally came, and every other day was a celebration. Highly qualified agriculturalists were hired to come and pioneer the college. The seven of us are the pioneers of Kushinga-Phikelela. Now it is a highly diversified College which includes agriculture and several other practical departments.

Trip to Mozambique

The tradition at UTC was, and still is, that the final year students had the privilege to choose where to go for an educational trip. Our class chose to go to Maputo in Mozambique. Mozambique got its independence in 1975 but was still as poor as ever. This was, to some of us, our second trip outside Zimbabwe having been to South Africa UNISA before. We stayed in churches that were not well organised. The shock we got upon entering some houses left us wondering what the Portuguese were up to when they left that country. Concrete cement was put in chambers and most amenity systems were vandalised. Blacks moved into dilapidated houses with just walls left some with man-made holes and cracks in them.

I for one was seeing the beach for the first time. Each time we went to the sea side I could not help but just put off my shoes and walk on the beach testing the salty waters of the Indian Ocean. Coming from a land locked country this experience was out of this world for me. UTC just spoiled us by opening the world to us. The exposure made us different pastors from that time onwards.

For the first time I saw some soldiers walking bare footed and in torn uniforms. Their Police Officers looked like some private security guards commanding very little respect. Zimbabwean fighters who had not yet returned after Independence treated local security personnel with contempt. But this was not their land, they were being hosted there. Perhaps the educational system/level in Mozambique was so low that foreigners, be they, other blacks or of European origin, could just trample on their hosts with disdain. I was not amused.

Some of us took time to visit homes and other places where Zimbabwean freedom fighters lived. Their accommodation ranged from relatively beautiful houses to barracks and warehouses they used as both for keeping things and also doubled as places to sleep. We were told that there were so many children there who had been fathered by Zimbabweans. That did not surprise us, as most often that is what happens in war situations. Local people were abused with impunity. If this is what happened at this far end on the coast what about in areas close to Zimbabwe where several thousands of our fighters were camped in preparation to cross over?

Formation of *Buriro/Esizeni/*Threshing Place

While I was still in college I had the privilege to be a founder member of *Buriro/Esizeni/*Threshing Place. This was a theological discussion forum formed by both lecturers, students of theology and clergy in ministry in their churches. It was ecumenical group comprising those interested ministers who were looking for a forum to do some theological reflection. We would spend weekends in various communities across the country conducting workshops with locals. It was really an eye opener. We discovered that rural folk had deep theological insights which were not being tapped. The group did not survive long because of the disturbances mainly in Matabeleland and Midlands because of the dissident problems. We had started very well but soon it was not safe for us to travel freely. By the end of the year I left UTC for my new station and I lost touch with the group. It did not survive long after I had left. Had we continued I think we would have traded in uncharted theological mine fields.

Back Home, First Appointment, Offered Juju

My maternal uncle, Mr Rabison Mukomba in Mhondoro, where I went to stay in 1973 was a traditional healer. His career was a very interesting one. One time he would be a very avowed medicinal practitioner of his trade in healing people. At another time he would renounce it and join a church. The time I left College he was at his peak in his trade. He sent word to me that I should visit his home before I took my first appointment to a circuit. Like any respectful *muzukuru*/nephew I obliged. In spite of my uncle's trade, I did not distance myself from him. I used to visit his home regularly. I always teased him about his trade, but we never lost our friendship. On this occasion he wanted to give me a special advice. He took me to his special hut where he practiced his healing and divining trade.

He was hesitating to say it all at first time. Finally, he alleged that many ministers of religion who came to his home area, including some Methodist clergy, came to him for help. This was perhaps to make me amenable to his advice that he wanted to offer me. He confessed that he did not give them bad magic. He gave them little potions of lion's nails and some other parts of dangerous animals which he alleged could make a leader strong and be feared and be respected by the people that they lead. In my case since I was still young in my late twenties, by when he felt I needed that juju more than my predecessors because of my youthfulness. In reply I told him the following true story.

In my final year at college me and my then lecturer, Rev F Chirisa, who, was twelve years older than me went with me for a funeral. Originally, we came from the same village, but we all left and now lived in very distant places. By having lived in one village both of us were bound to know or to be close to one or more other people who came from that village. One of his relatives had died in Highfield township of Harare. It happened that that person was also a distant relation of mine.

I went to inform him that I was going out of college to a funeral. When I told him where I was going he was keen because he was also preparing to drive to go to Highfield to his relative's funeral little did any of us know that. We were actually going to the same funeral. So, he took me there in his car.

Upon arrival, we were both welcomed very well. The ushers at the funeral showed us where to seat. I was given a more comfortable chair while Rev Chirisa was showed a rough log to sit on. He politely sat on the log. I deliberately sat on the chair but was sure something was going to happen. Rev Chirisa then called the guys who had offered us places to sit and asked the rationale they used to apportion us seats. The explanation was that I looked older than him therefore actually I deserved a more comfortable seat than his. He then went on to explain to them that I was twelve years his junior and, above all, I was his student. For the greater part of the time we were at the funeral people, could not just help but moved their eyes from him and then to me trying to make sense of what had expired.

I then said to uncle Robbi, "So, you see I do not need your juju. God has already bestowed upon me greatness which need not be spoiled by any earthly inducements."

He shook my hand and instead blessed me saying I should not forget that all people are equal and have to be respected. He was now convinced I did not need his juju. Before I left his hut, I stood up and said that all that I was seeing in that room were God's creation which we were manipulating to our selfish ends. Yes, he was making a living out of his trade but for me it was all cheating people. I was convinced though that some of his herbs worked very well. It was when it came to divination and other mysterious practices which I questioned. He was nevertheless a very nice man. I loved him, and he loved me and all his nephews.

CHAPTER SIX

MINISTERING IN MATABELELAND: STRUGGLES WITHIN A STRUGGLE

Went into a situation where one of us had refused to go

In December 1981 I was transported to Ndolwane Methodist House, in Nata Circuit. Ndolwane is about 100km from Plumtree, close to the border with Botswana. Plumtree is popularly known in *Kalanga* as *Titji tja Getjenge* but shortened as *Titji*. This simply meant Getjenge's Station. This was my first time to stay with people who were very different from my culture and language, a culture shock which helped me to appreciate other people. People in this area speak Kalanga at home while at church they use Ndebele. Even in schools they used Ndebele as the official language then.

The eight roomed Ndolwane manse had not been habited in twelve years. The last minister had left in 1968 and throughout the war of liberation, that is, 1964 to 1980, the place became dilapidated. No one looked after the place. The church there did not expect another minister to come. The semblance of a house became the place where goats from across the community came to sleep by night. There were only walls and nothing on the roof or windows. It was a ghost place fit for goats only.

The previous year a Methodist student, Rev Glorious Chombo, from college had been sent there by the church. After arriving at Ndolwane he made up his mind to come back to the church and tender his resignation. He was a very brilliant student. He proceeded to enrol at the University of Zimbabwe and furthered his education. The idea of the church was that the minister who is posted there was the one who would supervise the rebuilding of the manse. When I was posted there, most people thought I was going to resign too. I decided to make a maiden journey with my heavily pregnant wife who was expecting our first child. Upon seeing the place, we decided that she would come back to Harare to give birth while I soldiered on with the rebuilding. There was no toilet. The conditions were just bad for someone expecting.

Around mid-December, I travelled back to Bulawayo to accompany a Johnson and Fletcher Lorry full of building materials, to the last nail, paint and everything. The 'quantity man' had done a good job. He was given the house plan and he had ordered all that was needed to resuscitate the house.

The lorry left Bulawayo after 4pm and we arrived at Ndolwane around 10pm. Little did I know that we were going to battle with some goats whose home was the disused manse. We had an hour of running battles with the goats. Fortunately, the local builder, one Mr Sibindi, came to our rescue when he heard the lorry arriving he rushed to meet with us. There were drums lying around which he was going to use for building. We would chase goats from one room and then put a drum to stop them from coming in. We did the same with the other three entrances to the house. The goats would return and jump through the window openings until they got tired and left. Never did they come back. That was my baptism at Ndolwane.

After about 14 days, I was staying in a modern house with everything that a house needed. It became the best house in the community. Our neighbours had not proper shelter. They were the local *Sili*/bushmen people who only had one shelter each but with large families. They put big fires in the shelter throughout the night for warmth. At times the women would come to our windows, even the bedroom window asking for sugar or bread. We were coming from a place where no one dared approach a house through the window. In this area the people would actually knock on the window and then just make a sign pointing at their mouth. Then you knew they were asking for food. They knew we did not understand their language.

In these 14 days we were sleeping on door frames together with the builder with the moonlight watching over us before the roof was mounted. It was an experience of its own. One night the builder discovered that I did not have *nduku*, (a knob Kerry). Traditionally people from this area sleep with a *nduku* besides their bed for protection. The next day he took me to the bush and he made one for me which I would take with me to the UK in the future when opportunity arose for me to go for further studies. Before we ate food, the builder would take a morsel of food and put it on the ground. Upon asking him why he did that he explained that it was for the ancestors. After eating he would take back the morsel onto the plate. Little by little I was learning local culture which I appreciated so much.

Special Welcome

One early morning I left Ndolwane on my motor bike to travel to Plumtree/Titji. It was very clear, for the sun was just about to rise. The road passed through the bush. As I was about to finish the bush I saw something that appeared like a very big dog. I just wondered what kind of a big dog like this one. It had a big hump with lots of furs. I was afraid and just felt my legs getting numb. I only managed to drive to the nearby homestead. Luckily owner of the home had just woken up and was going daily work. He saw me coming towards him and recognized me as the new minister. *"Uyangapi ekuseni kungaka?"* he asked. (Where are you going so early in the morning?) He noticed I was puzzled so he enquired further. I told him about what I saw describing exactly what type of animal that crossed ahead of me.

The man took me into his house and sat down with me and explained what had happened. He told me that what I had seen was a 'lion' (*mhondoro*) an extra territorial animal that is believed to be the 'custodian' of the community. In local tradition, once a new person saw that lion, it meant that that person was very welcome. So, he said I had been welcomed by the local spirits. In his words he said, "there is nothing to fear any more from now onwards. The owners of this land have welcomed you. Be free to do your work *Mufundisi*-minister."

My strength came back and after a while I proceeded with my journey. That experience is still very fresh in my mind each time I think of it.

My First Day Driving a Car

My church was so kind to me. I was one of those lucky ones who was given a motor bike to use for my work in the circuit. For the first few weeks in Nata I used the bike quite often and I used to fall off it regularly. One white farmer a Mr Oosthuissen used to see me in bandages on my face and arms. Little did I know that he was feeling pity for me each time I passed through his garage. One day when I went straight into his garage, that became his opportunity to pass his sympathy. He quickly offered to exchange his nice car for my bike. I could not believe my ears. I asked him to repeat the offer, which he did. I asked for a call for me to phone my Church Headquarters for I had not finished paying for it the bike.

The President of the church was very supportive of the idea but warned me to check if he was not a cone-man. His car was a well-kept Citron DS 20. Indeed, it was in good shape and I just could not believe my fortune.

When the Church gave me a go-ahead we spent the day working on the paper work. We did not finish that day, but he allowed me to drive the car back to Ndolwane, about 100 km away. I had never driven a car before in my life. I did not even have a close relative who had a car. Seating by the driver's side was on rare occasions if I got a ride in one.

I had never dreamt of having a car of my own. If I had had a clue to possess one in the future I could have observed how drivers did it on the wheel. Come this day I was bold enough to have a go at it. Around 4pm Mr Oosthuissen wondered if it was wise for me to drive alone. He asked me if I had driven before to which I answered in the positive. I thought since I had a class three licence for motor bikes it would be easy for me to drive the car. He gave me the keys.

Upon starting the car, I rammed into a petrol tank at my back, as the car was in reverse gear. Mr Oosthuissen came to my rescue. He pulled the car from the garage and left me on the road. I then had a go at it driving with the hand break on and in first gear only. When I tried to put it into second gear it was failing to pull. One thought said it was a dis-functional car, but I decided to go on. One man from Ndolwane saw me driving and the car was producing some smoke from the wheels because it was binding since the hand break was on. He stopped me and discovered that the hand break was on. He released it and then the car started to pull. This was the beginning of my driving night mares.

A motor bike then had three gears, so I drove the car like one. I could only go to third gear all the way to Ndolwane about 100km. When you drive a car for the first time, I discovered that the car looked like it was somehow deformed. In that corner, I felt like the car was not straight. When I came to the first bridge, I just could not fathom how I was going to cross it. I stopped the car, went out of the car, to make sure I was in the middle of the road then got back and drove across the bridge. That was to be the ritual at each bridge I crossed. I would stop the car and make sure I was spot on before crossing. Thank God the road had no other traffic and up to Ndolwane I never met a car. My wife could not believe it when I pulled the car behind our manse. We were to use the car for the next two and half years until we left the country and left it with my brother who used it for the next three years.

CHAPTER SEVEN

FAMILY TRAGEDY

My brother Christopher, who was a policeman had been promoted to be the rank of a Sergeant. He had worked in the police force since 1971, at both Murewa 80km north of Harare and 65km Marondera east of Harare Police Stations. This time he was in Marondera before he was promoted. Soon after promotion he was posted to Masvingo 300km south of Harare. He never reached there. On the way, after Chivhu, he started seeing things in his vision. Because of his awkward behaviour, those accompanying him decided not to proceed with the journey. He was taken home. The whole family did not know how to handle the situation. Our mother had died the previous year.

When he was normal again he liked to confess of something he had done. He told the family that he picked a snuff container which we call *nhekwe* in Hwedza area. And he thought this was sent by our ancestors. What had happened earlier when I stayed with him in Murewa was that he used to complain that he failed to tell how he used his money. He was always in credit. He was broke on the day he received his salary. He would go to the shops and open accounts and at the end of the month all the money would go to his food account. So, he decided to go to a diviner.

He was told that there was a spirit in our family which wanted to be 'welcomed' and we were refusing its gesture. He was told that he was one of the candidates, himself and a cousin brother of ours who was the son of my father's elder brother. When he came across the nhekwe, for him, that was a confirmation that he was the one appointed. He would then say to us. This *nhekwe* was the one which had invited this calamity in our home.

My mother's younger sister, Aunt Francisca took over as our custodian mother. (They were six in their family, Mrs Zomuya, Teresa my mother, Rabison, Francisca, Monica and George). She took him to Harare to her home. They tried to send him to all sorts of helpers until they finally decided to take him back home.

They arrived at home in the afternoon and made food for him and others and at night went to sleep. While Aunt Francisca remained in the kitchen talking through the night with two close female relatives. He came back into the kitchen and sat by the fading fire. He just took a log and hit aunt Francisca on the head and she fell down instantly. When she was transported to Chivhu hospital she died on the way. Our father went through hell that night. My brother was immediately arrested. The funeral went on but there were lots of demands to our family as tradition demands in such occurrences. Finally, aunt Monica was buried at her home in Mhondoro.

Naturally relations between children of my mother and aunt Monica's children were in tatters. I only arrived from Plumtree when she had been buried. I did not witness the commotion that took place at the funeral. Christopher was tried and found to have been mentally derailed. He was sent to Mlondolozi prison in Bulawayo where such prisoners were kept. For years he was to be in that prison. But he turned to Christ while there. He took many religious courses and he passed them very well. Meanwhile I was now managing his affairs with his wife at home. We built him a nice home with the funds released by the government towards his pension. He was finally released in 1989. When he was now a born-again Christian. The mental disturbances would be on and off albeit after a long time. I remember very well that when he relapsed he would be sent to my work place at Chivero and I would be responsible for bathing him during the absence of his wife.

His wife was a strong 'bloused' Methodist Ruwadzano/Manyano member. Upon his release he wanted to join the Church, but he believed that the Methodist Church was not strong enough to help him through the turmoil he was going through. He joined Bethsaida Church, an Apostolic Church and he really felt at home there.

Bethsaida Church was started by a former Methodist Evangelist Mr Loveness Manhango in the mid-1950s. Together with Evangelist Paul Mwazha the Apostle of Africa, these two vibrant Methodists left the church because they felt the Holy Spirit was being muzzled within his ranks. They began as soul mates but later separated and formed their churches which are some of the fastest growing indigenous churches in Zimbabwe. Ironically both Apostle Mwazha and Archbishop Manhango still claim to be true Methodists. Should anyone deny that? What they did and continue to do is what the Wesley brothers did. Interestingly they both hail from the same area in Chivu where I also come from. They take me as one of their products each time I come across them. And I do not deny that. I admire the two and take them as examples of followers of Christ. Their dedication is out of this world.

My brother did not look back. He was very strict in his faith. He died in 2010 when he was Mufundisi/minister in the Bethsaida church. His funeral was graced by many evangelists, ministers and bishops of his church. Archbishop Manhango sent a representative because he was not well at the time. My brother's funeral was one of those rare religious occasions. Every action that was taken at the funeral was interpreted religiously. Even the last ceremony which they do after 40 days of mourning was just out of this world. I wished if their teaching on death could be emulated by other churches including mine.

Local Traditions never ceased to amaze me - Ndolwane

One day I went to this section of my Church. In that area of our work we had local church leaders who looked after big 'sections' which included a number of 'societies'. There was this lady who was in charge of keeping records, including Sunday's records of offerings. It could take me a while before I went to collect the money from her. On this particular day, I arrived from another church service. The woman had been waiting for me for some time. When I arrived, she took me aside and opened her bag. In it there was another piece of cloth in which was tied some money for safe keeping. As she opened she made sure I was watching. Little did she realise that she had a traditional *muti*/herb which have some powers. In Shona it's called *chifumuro* in Kalanga it is known as *sifumulo*. This muti was on top of the money. As soon as she noticed it, she apologised to me. It fell off and I picked it up for her. She was very much embarrassed. I knew what was going on in her mind. Normally *chifumuro* works in private. It should not be displayed to others. Worse still, it had been seen by her minister. I tried to console her by saying that it was herself that was keeping the herb and not vice versa. We both laughed over it and then prayed together.

The burial of a Headman

The local chief had a number of headmen under him. One day one of the local headman, a Mr Sibindi died uncle to my builder. He was not a church goer, but I was invited to bury him. That was my first burial ceremony in that area. An ox was slaughtered for meat for the mourners. When time to bury the body came I was not amused. First, they destroyed the hut at the back and the body was brought out through that opening. The body was wrapped in the ox's skin. Imagine the wet skin and a body inside it! These two did not just jelly. They tried to tie the body with ropes while inside the skin, but it was a mammoth task. He was to be buried somewhere nearby, in the cattle kraal actually. A short while after the burial, it was like we had not put anything in the kraal. Cattle were allowed to sleep in it that very night. Sitting with the elders, I sought to know why all that was done at the funeral went that way. I was informed, and I started to appreciate our cultural differences.

Comparing this funeral with those in my home area this was no funeral at all. In my area funerals, border on being some kind of orgies. Mourners are treated to much beer and food. There is a lot of singing yet in this place it is a sombre event. In Mashonaland, it is more than a celebration, mixed with weeping and all sorts of noises. There is a lot of drumming especially at night when mourners dance the night away. Such was my confusion for I had not come across such practices before. If the locals were to attend our funerals they would think we were not serious. On the other hand, the seriousness shown in Kalangaland does not appeal to Shona mourners. The Shona are a people who sing always, they sing when they work, when they are angry, when they are happy and when they are sad.

Surprise – surprise

One day I was in Titji and I met this man who was a local preacher of long standing. What did I note on his jacket? He had a Zimbabwe National Traditional Healers Association (ZINATHA) badge on. I made some investigations, lest I had mistaken him for our man when he was not. I looked for someone else in Titji who came from that same area. It was not a problem at all because most of the time many people from around Titji spent some time there. Indeed, my fears were confirmed. He was the President of the local Chapter of ZINATHA. I just wondered how he managed to juggle around between being a Local Preacher in the church and a President of a Local Chapter of traditional healers. For the locals this was not an issue at all. He was providing a very important services to the community. As a result, everybody in the community respected him.

As if that was not enough, the President of the Methodist Church then Rev C.C Makuzva was visiting our circuit that month. I went to meet him at Matjinge, at the Superintendent's place which is very near to Plumtree. I did put up there that night. Early the next morning, the president woke me up and gave me badza/ a hoe to take to the bush with him to dig some roots and barks of various trees there. Little did I know that my Superintendent Minister, the Rev E. Chidemo, knew that each time the President came to visit, he took back with him different kinds of herbs which he picked up from the local forests. We spent the better part of the morning digging in the nearby bush. At the end of the search, he had a boot full of these different types of herbs. I was just a 'probationer', by that time not yet ordained, and I was seeing these things. I just wondered if he did not have contacts with our Local Preacher mentioned above, for he lived very close to Matjinge. I later learnt that Rev Makuzva helped so many people with his herbs including some of our senior ministers who had chronic diseases like asthma etc. At one time I visited his home and saw what looked like a pharmacy in one of his rooms. Indeed, he was a "chemist par-excellence".

CHAPTER EIGHT

IMPOSITION OF A CURFEW, 1982 -83

Since 1981 when I went with my family to serve as a Church minister at Ndolwane Methodist Church in Plumtree, in Matabeleland South. We were received very well by the Kalanga people in Ndolwane we had enjoyed the love and care that we received from both the Christians and well-wishers who lived at Ndolwane. However, 1982-87 was one of the worst periods in the history of Zimbabwe politically. This was the time when the infamous 'Gukurahundi', North Korea trained Brigade swept throughout the Matabeleland region took place. The political situation in this region made our stay very difficult. A curfew was imposed in order to curb the free movement of people and the so-called dissidents. We were told that the dissidents wanted to discredit the government by kidnapping and killing whites, government employees and the Shonas. There was no security for these three groups of people. As a result, government employees were only allowed to move around with security forces and whites never came to the area. What was also funny about the dissidents was that there were not worried about the Shonas who were not married. They wanted to abduct families so that they could ask for what they wanted from the government. Some of the soldiers had the audacity to advise us to leave the area because, then, they could not see the situation improving.

The Midlands and both Matabeleland North and South Provinces of the country were shocked to have curfew imposed on them. This was done to curb the movements of the so-called 'dissidents'. For the first six months, we could not travel freely, but far. The second part of the year, the conditions of the curfew had changed. One day, I took a wheelbarrow to fetch water from the clinic borehole which was about 800m from the manse. As I was nearing the manse pushing the wheel barrow I was accosted by a soldier who instructed me to leave it there. There was this heavy container full of water. I was told that the new laws now prohibited anyone both from using wheel barrows or scotch carts. I was forced to carry the container on my head only to come back to push an empty wheel barrow. No one was allowed to travel except when one applied for a permit to travel. One had to go to the local camp of soldiers and had to put his/her case and start the process of applying to for a travel permit.

Abandoned my clerical clothes

The situation at Ndolwane was just that one had to be innovative to survive. The first thing I did was to buy an 'overall' to use when going for pastoral work whenever I had the opportunity, to do so, that was before the curfew was imposed. With my newly acquired knob-Kerry, it just endeared me so well with the locals. I actually became one of them. We also acquired a brown dog which we gave the name *Kuseka/ Ukuhleka*, loosely translated, 'laughing'.

This dog grew to be a wonderful pet. It just loved us as a family. People who came to our house just loved the dog. It played with everyone. It accompanied me on my local trips too. However, I often got into problems when my dog arrived first and met with dislike from other dogs. It would quickly coil its tail to prove that it was harmless. In other instances, locals would tell that the pastor was around once they saw my dog but there were times when it ventured into the villages on its own like any other dog would do. Some locals would then ask me why I did not call at their homes since they had seen my dog. I would always be at pain to explain it came on its own.

Putting on clerical clothes could have made me a stranger and even feel out of place. I only put on clerical clothes when I was travelling to Titji or to Bulawayo or beyond. I also looked for the simplest of shoes in order to look like the locals. In the process I learnt a lot of their language. The confusion was that there were three languages to master at one time, Kalanga, Ndebele and the 'Sili' language, which had more 'clicks' that Ndebele. In many of these places you would come across people who knew Shona very well and most then were no good at all to me because they conversed with me in Shona even if I protested. At one congregation where there was no interpreter I was asked to preach in Shona and they all said they followed my service very well.

Witness to the Genocide in Matabeleland

Ndolwane is situated in Matabeleland South Province of Zimbabwe where Mugabe sent the Fifth Brigade, a North Korean trained brigade to fight the so-called dissidents in 1983. I was there until August 1984. As such I am a 'first-hand, witness to a genocide which was so gruesome that many people were killed. On one trip to Plumtree we arrived at Bhagani and there were hordes of soldiers. One soldier pulled open the door of the bus and stood by the entrance. He started shouting in Shona, instructing people to produce their IDs. The bus was over-full. One young man sitting close to where I was, right at the back responded saying, *Kasizwel*'meaning we hear nothing'. The soldier ordered all of us to disembark. We were lined up and just over 30 young men were selected and that was the last time we saw them. Some of these young people were children of some of my members at church. This was only one of the many incidents that I was going to witness.

On the 18th of September 1982 I wrote a letter to the then President of the Methodist Church, Rev Caspen C. Makuzwa informing him about the situation that we were living in. Below is the letter I wrote:

Dear Sir

I write to inform you about our position here at Ndolwane. The situation has suddenly changed because of the curfew which was imposed to curb the movement of 'dissidents'. We are increasingly becoming afraid as each day passes because of the stories being told here, about the dissidents. So, our nights here are very unpleasant. One night, in spite of the curfew we had stones thrown on our roof and we wondered who was doing that, yet people were not supposed to be moving around by then.

We, however, enjoy the love and the care of both the Christians and other well-wishers around here. But what is said about the 'dissidents' is that they want to discredit the government by using sinister methods of kidnapping and killing 'whites', government officials and the Shonas. Of all these three groups we are the only ones without any kind of protection. The government employees move about with security and the whites do not come here. So those left without protection are us the Shonas. They do not bother the Shonas who are married here. They want a complete set so that when they abduct a family they will ask what they want from the government. This is what we hear these days. Even some of the soldiers who are here advise us to leave because they do not see the situation improving.

WE like this place very much – but I am afraid that we are now scared. Unless the situation improves soon we may face danger.

Faithfully yours

Rev L.T.C. Kadenge

NB: 1 Cor. 10 vs. 12 and 13 reads: "So if you think you are standing, watch out that you do not fall. No testing has overtaken you that is not common to everyone. God is faithful, and he will not let you be tested beyond your strength, but with the testing he will also provide the way out so that you may be able to endure it."

From that day onwards, we ignored the disturbances. We became stronger and courageous and nothing happened to us.

At one time, a fact finding, group of journalists came to our area with the Deputy Commander of the Army the late Solomon Mujuru. I was prepared to go and testify what I had witnessed. I only heard on the radio that the mission had come and gone back and that all the clergy had come and presented their complaints. By 'all clergy' I later learnt they meant Catholic priests. This left me baffled and I felt very isolated, yet I was one of those in the thick of things.

Praying for rains during severe drought periods

During the 1980s the Matabeleland region experienced a life-threatening drought. We had to help the people whose lives were put on the line by a severe drought. However, I arranged a prayer meeting with both the political and religious leadership of the Ndolwane area. On the 18th of January in 1984, I wrote a letter to the Headmaster of a nearby school so that he could announce the proposed prayer meeting to school children at the assembly so that they could take the massage home to their parents. Here is a copy of the letter;

> Ndolwane Methodist Church
> P.O Box 198
> Plumtree
> 18th January 1984

The Headmaster

Dear Sir,

Could you please help by telling the children the following information so that they tell their parents?

(a) In view of the current drought we are thinking of putting our heads together as residents of this area and pray for the rains.

(b) A working committee comprising of the leaders of the Zionists, Apostles, The Seventh Day Adventists and the Methodists will meet on Friday 20-01-84 at Matiwaza Methodist Church at 2.00pm. Those who have not been notified but who are leaders of any worshiping people are asked to come to this Friday meeting which will draw up an agenda for the proposed Sunday Prayer meeting by all people.

(c) The proposed day for the prayer is Sunday 22-01-84 starting from 11.00am at Matiwaza.

(d) The prayer meeting will be led by all the leaders of the worshiping community. All those present will participate as the spirit directs.

We are in no way suggesting that the Lord has forgotten us, but we are sure that He also wants us to tell Him of our needs. We have looked at our cattle and ourselves in this dire need and feel that God alone can see us through.

All people are invited to this important meeting.

Yours Sincerely

Levee T.C. Kadenge (Rev)

Many people came for the prayer meeting that I had organized. We had a spiritually lifting and a very prayerful moment. God answered our prayers and we received plenty of rains thereafter. This clearly showed us that God will always love his people. The unity that the people of Ndolwane showed on that occasion was so overwhelming that became one occasion that I will never forget in my life. The importance of this occasion lies in the fact that the Church, including all the denominations, managed to join hands to fight poverty and hunger. The other lesson that I got from this crucial event is that the Church has the ability to work together (in unison).

Invited to a Traditional Ceremony

The then chief, Chief Ndolwane, who was also a Local Preacher in the Methodist Church, invited me to a traditional ceremony at Matiwaza just 3km away from where I stayed. I borrowed a bicycle and cycled together myself and the chief. We went there just after our church service which ended around 1pm. The people there treated us as special guests since I was with the chief. I did not know what to expect for it was my first time to attend such functions.

It was 'a home-coming' ceremony for some two traditional healers who had just graduated. In this area the practice was that those who aspire to become traditional healers would go through a very rigorous selection process which ends with them going to distant places to train under the supervision of some designated individual experts who would either pass or fail them. The two ladies in question had been sent to Botswana, just across the border, for their training and had gone through the training successfully. This day was set apart for the celebrations to welcome them back and celebrate the success.

While most people sat on home-made stools, logs and bricks the two of us, the chief and I were given high chairs to sit on. The dance started soon after our arrival. I had never seen such a dance. It was just out of this world. The dancers just put all their effort into it. They were scantly-dressed in *magavu* tied to their feet, as accompanying instruments which made some very melodious music. I could not help but just follow the music with keen interest. At one point I stood up, in excitement only to be pulled down by the chief who thought the locals would not understand my motive. I had joined in the clapping of hands and moving my body to the rhythms of the song.

Then came break-time. Having passed the 'exams' at the trainer's place was not enough. The healers had to be tested locally too. Someone hid an item and the newly graduated healers were asked to look for it. Once they got it everybody shouted out in joy and dance started again. True to tradition they hunted for the items and picked them. I never witnessed such frenzy like I saw that day. As the dance continued some food was served to everybody. For the first time I ate the local traditional food called *umcanca* – that is maize cooked together with a type of pumpkin that tastes so, very nice.

Guess whom did I see there? Most of our church members who did not come to church that day were there. Some of them had difficulty in taking part because I was there. Others were watching what I was up to hence the wise counsel from the chief for me not to stand up and be seen. After a while my people, as it were, relaxed and took part here and there. But I am sure they could have been freer if I was not there. I really enjoyed the occasion, though, and wished if there was another one to come sooner.

Seeking help for the Silis

Near the station where I was ministering from, there was a group of people who are locally referred to as the Silis' or bushmen. The Silo people used to have very large families, normally with 6 to 11 children per family. Most of them used to stay in the bush and very few stayed along the road. They were good hunters but because of the '*Gukurahundi*' atrocities their hunting activities had come to a standstill. A good number of the men were then employed by the locals to be herd boys. Their pay was either in cash or in kind. As a result, they were exploited by the local people. One striking factor was that both the ordinary and well to do people were so used to the suffering of the *Sili* people that they simply accepted them as a suffering community. However, any visitor to the area would be moved by the lifestyle that the Silis were leading. To crown it all, this minority group of people was living in abject poverty. They did not have food, clothes and proper shelter. They relied on hunting for meat and root gathering. They also survived on asking for food from the Kalangas. I felt for them. As part of my service to the people, I approached Christian Care, a Service arm of the Zimbabwe Council of Churches, to solicit assistance specifically for the Silis people.

In response to my visit to their offices the Christian Care officers provided the *Sili* people with blankets. Below is a letter that I received from Rev S.K Manguni who was the then co-ordinator of the Christian Care activities in the area;

27 June 1984

Rev L.T.C Kadenge

Ndolwane Methodist Church

C/o Dulini Store

P.O. Ndolwane,

Bulawayo

My reply was prompt

Dear Revd Manguni

Thank you for your letter dated 27 June 1984.

I am glad that you have decided to pursue the Silis' plight. Below is some information about these forgotten lovely people.

I have personally met a few of them but there are so many of them near the border. A rough estimate of the men only is well over 200. They have large families of 6 to 11 children per family. Though they stay in the bush, the largest percentage stay along the road.

They are good hunters. Their hunting activities are now nil, because of the situation. I always see them carrying traditional tools. The 'up-to-date' ones sell stools and *komanis*, which they make from certain trees in the bush. They drink heavily, whatever intoxicating drink they come across and this includes most women.

They survive by asking for food from the Kalangas. A good number of men are somehow employed by the locals to look after their cattle. The payment is either in kind or in cash. Those paid in cash do not get anything more than $20.00 per month. Those paid in kind get one calf at the end of the year and some goodies which are given at the discretion of the employer. In a way these people are exploited. I know a good number of people who work in town and in South Africa and some who have businesses who exploit these poor people in this way.

They now eat maize and the normal vegetables. Their meat ranges from fatty animals down even to the diseased ones or those which die on their own. They do not choose when it comes to relish. Most of them sleep around fires for warmth.

I have also come across a family eating '*butu* – *Mhunga's* waste. As I write I have two large families who looked to us as their main suppliers of both food and clothing. These are our neighbours who happen to be Silis.

The only suggestion which I can firmly make is that your Officer comes here so that we discuss with the people concerned. The Headman, who is Kalanga has accepted the idea whole-heartedly. He volunteered to help in gathering these people if we want them to come together. I was suggesting that this Officer comes before I leave this place. I leave on 28 July for studies in the UK. By this I am not saying that he cannot come after I have left. If your programme is so tight, I will arrange with the Headman and the Evangelist who is to take my place so that they work with the Officer in trying to help these unfortunate people. But I see the matter as urgent.

One striking factor is that the ordinary people including the well to do people here are so used to the suffering of the Silis that they have accepted them as a suffering community. But any visitor or sympathetic person will be moved by their hard life which is deprived of the basics of life. Any progressive Sili is automatically cut off from the *Silis* and he is accepted either as a Kalanga or Ndebele as the case maybe. Some adopt the *Zibongos* – totems of their masters.

If the Officer is coming before I leave this place, please inform me even at short notice. I am not on the phone – but my wife is on the phone at her work place at Ndolwane Hospital which in less than 800 meters from our house – phone 00122 Plumtree. They check in at 7.30am and knock off at 4.30pm in most cases. If he is using a car and hesitates to drive up here I can meet him in Plumtree at the Post Office and accompany him to this place which is about 100km North-North East of Plumtree, on dust road, which is an average road. This means that I will board a bus from here early in the morning and it gets to Plumtree between 9am and 10am daily. I suggest accompanying the Officer because soldiers may harass him if he is alone. He should carry with him his identification including those for employment.

I only hope this letter is not confusing because of its length.

Waiting for your rescue

Your sincerely

Rev L.T.C Kadenge

After compiling all the details that the Christian Care wanted from me they quickly came in to assist the Sili people. It is my firm belief that genuine Christianity is about sharing. It is also the duty of a Church minister to look for the means of survival for the poor.

Each time I used my car I had to apply for permission

A typical letter would look like the one below;

The Chief Inspector

Zimbabwe republic Police (Sup.Unit)

Khame rest Camp

Matabeleland South

Dear Sir

I am applying for a road permit for road travel to Plumtree on the 22nd February 1984. I understand I must get a return road permit from the Sub-Joc Plumtree.

Here are my particulars; Employer: The Methodist Church in Zimbabwe, My personal Identity number – 29-007511 C -18.

I will be using my car with the registration No 9426 V. The last date I used a road permit was on the 11th February 1984 which I was given at Plumtree.

Thank you

Yours sincerely

Rev Levee T.C Kadenge

I was to be away for a month. Our second child, a daughter named *Chiedza* was born on 7 March 1984. Two weeks later we had to take her back to Ndolwane, a journey of about 600km from Harare. On my way back, I was so frustrated that I wrote back to the church President:

Dear Sir

I write to inform you that we arrived at Ndolwane on 20th of March. We did not have a safe journey. The experience that we went through on this last journey of ours was very nasty and inhumane at times. We were treated with utmost disrespect. We went through nine road blocks from Bulawayo to Ndolwane. To crown it all, the soldiers nearly shot us all on our arrival at Ndolwane. One of the car windows was covered with cloth to shield the children from the direct heat of the sun. These soldiers suspected that we were hiding someone in the car. They rushed to our car which had just arrived and accused us of having let someone into the house before their arrival. They tried to destroy the door as I pleaded with them that we were still looking for the keys to open the door. Guns were being pointed at us as other comrade soldiers were busy kicking the door and calling for more soldiers to come. The whole family was in tears crying while I was trying to explain to them why we came and that we were given the permission to drive in our car.

We did well, just to come without enquiring first by telephone because if we had done that we were not going to come back here. The situation has deteriorated, even though there were not contacts with dissidents in this area. The situation intensifies with the change of soldiers. When a new group of soldiers come they come with their own ideas and want to start afresh with their own investigations and disregard what others had done. So, the situation does not improve.

What worries us is the accusation which is levelled at us. We are asked why we are here and why we seem to be not worried. They say this proves that we are in good books with dissidents. We always tell them that we just do not know what we will say to the dissidents when they come to us. We are also afraid. But they do not accept this.

We will stay here if we are not forced to move but we are afraid that there are some soldiers who want to take the law into their hands. They said they were going to make investigations and they will come back to us. They really do not accept that we can stay here without the approval of the 'dissidents'.

We need your support in prayers

Yours in His Service

Levee

What was happening was that soldiers did not stay in one place for more than two weeks. So, each time the soldiers were transferred after every two weeks. Apparently, there was fighting in Mozambique currently and our soldiers were also operating in that country. These were the soldiers who would come and terrorise people like they were in Mozambique. I never saw a dissident myself, but many people were slaughtered just because they were either Ndebele/Kalanga or Silis.

One day I confronted a soldier who had come close to me. We had travelled together to the border because they did not know the short cut near Maitengwe Dam. I asked the man when there were the two of us alone why they were so brutal. He told me that they were coming from a real war situation in Mozambique and they did not trust any Ndebele speaking person. Each time they came across young Ndebele men they suspected them to be dissidents hence they just killed them rather than want to investigate. After two weeks they were back to Mozambique and a new group comes and does the same. From Mozambique they were told they were fighting a similar war in Zimbabwe hence the cruelty.

Educating the people

In June 1984 I donated a few books to George Silinduka High School in Nyamandlovu about 60km north-west of Ndolwane. I did this because I believed, and I still believe, that education is the only key to success in any society. To develop a society, one must develop the human factor first. At the centre of development are the people. I also think that education is a human right that every child in this world should enjoy.

Establishment of a Secondary School at Ndolwane

An idea of opening a secondary school in the area was muted. Since this was my area of passion, I quickly supported the idea. Little did I know that it was a political 'hot potato'. I went for it naively yet there were some who did not want it to be built at Ndolwane. My coming in to support the idea was taken as high-jacking' the project for it to be near me. Indeed, Ndolwane was the ideal place for the school but there was a powerful person who came from another area called Butje and he wanted it to be there. Thus, I was accused of wanting to do things 'the Shona way'. The Shonas in that part of the country were known as *maBambazonke*, literally meaning one who takes everything.

I had to quickly pull out, for the labelling was getting too far. I was now being taken as a sell-out. I however left before the school was built. The school was eventually built at Ndolwane and I was informed it became very popular to the extent that a 'bush boarding school' developed quickly.

Forced to Buy a Party Card

Zimbabwean politics after independence have always been characterized by cohesion. At the end of 1982, word came to people in Matabeleland that everyone should buy ZAN-PF party card. Because of fear everyone had to find means to go and buy one or else face the consequences of not buying one. The cards could only be bought in Plumtree about 100km away. You had to go there in person to buy. Imagine, even those people who had never been to Plumtree and had no reason to go there had to this time around. The cost to travel was also prohibitive.

I had initially resisted but later found out that the card was demanded at road blocks and if you did not have one then you were labelled a sell-out. Being perceived as a sell-out was a serious matter. You could easily be killed. The day I finally went to Plumtree for the card was a nightmare. Our bus arrived a bit late in the morning. We found out that the cards had been finished for they were in great demand. There was no way I could go back without the card. I ended up sleeping in a queue for the card because we had been promised that the other batch of cards was on its way from Harare. I had never had a political party card in my life before even though I had voted for R.G. Mugabe in 1980. This time around it was a directive that everyone should carry one. The card was one's passport literally when travelling in the country.

Even though everybody bought a party card the party ZANU-PF lost the elections there in Ndolwane to ZAPU-PF. The party never got a single seat in that area. Matabeleland North and South were a very stronghold of ZAPU PF area. Forcing people to buy the ruling party cards did not change anything at all.

Forced to walk 45km

One day I decided to go to Plumtree to see the Social Welfare Services Officers on behalf of one of our members who was not getting his payout. Mr Mongwa was a blind man who used to get some money from the Social Welfare Department. I approached the Police Station at Ndolwane and was given permission to ride on the army truck which was going to take some provisions from Plumtree. I boarded the truck in the morning. It was full of people most of who had serious business to take care of in this small town. When we arrived at Bhagani we were met with by a group of soldiers who were in no compromising mood. They stopped the lorry and ordered us all to return to Ndolwane on foot. We had travelled about 45km. There was no explanation as to why we had to go back. We started on our way back around 9am and arrived back at Ndolwane just after 3pm. We went through a police station called Madlembudzi. The punishment was just uncalled for. It was my first and last time to travel those bushy places along the Botswana-Zimbabwe border.

Finished my first-degree B. Th with UNISA

I wrote my last UNISA examination in Plumtree in 1982 and passed all the 8 modules I had been left with. I finished my degree in three years-time together with my colleague Rev C. Matsikiti, who had started a year earlier. I always look to Ndolwane as my first 'university college'. Most of the time there I had little to do because of the curfew that was imposed in that area, so I spent most of my time reading and writing my assignments.

At the end of 1983, I got a letter from the Church's Head Office instructing me to write a letter to Britain, thanking the World Church Office there for offering me a scholarship to study at Bristol University. I later learnt that when the scholarship came we had to fight it out again between me and my colleague. Fortunately, we were both not there. The offer landed on me without our knowledge of what was happening. I did write to the British Conference of the Methodist Church thanking them for the scholarship. I was to leave for studies in September the following year.

Paid Half Salary

For the two and a half years I was stationed at Ndolwane I only got half my salary. Nata is a very dry place and support of church work is just not there. The church treated Nata as 'a mission post' which was assisted with half the salary of whoever went there. I knew the arrangement but hoped that the circuit would pay the remainder. For me, it was very clear that the circuit was unable to meet its obligations. I had to be content with the half that I was getting from the head office. At that time. I was supposed to get Zimbabwe dollars, $120.00. The Connexional Office maintained its $60.00 without fail.

It was only in 1988 when I had come back from studies abroad that I decide to write a very strong letter to the church wanting to know if it was my fault that I did not get my other part of the salary. The church decided to compensate me but, in a way, it dictated. I was owing the church a loan of the motor bike it had given me. So, the $1920.00 I was owed was put to my account. I was cleared of my credit with the church. If I had not fought to get that money I am sure that was going to be the end of it.

CHAPTER NINE

ANOTHER CULTURE SHOCK

By September we arrived in the UK. First, we were in London for a week at the Methodist Guest House. We enjoyed seeing London for the first time. What we discovered was that even if London was the most populated place we had ever stayed in, we were shocked by how lonely people could be. Apart from the guest house, we could not communicate with anyone. Not that our English was bad but because no one talked to anyone. You went into a super market and made your shopping, went to the till, you see the amount on the till and you pay and leave without saying a word. Even if you said thank you that was that. No wonder why most foreigners, among them a few Zimbabweans ended in psychiatric units because of stress. One young man came back to Zimbabwe with mental problems because of loneliness. You are rubbing shoulders with people in trains and buses, but you do not talk to them. This makes someone get mad. I made a fatal mistake one day and greeted someone I did not know. They nearly called the police because I was interfering in their privacy.

After a week in London, we left for Birmingham where we were to spend two weeks while we were being orientated into British life. The period we were in Birmingham, at Selly Oak College was memorable. The College trains missionaries who are in transit to foreign lands. Those coming into UK are also inducted into British life at this college.

There were a few us from various parts of the world on the same scholarship programme. As foreigners we found reason to talk to each other all the time. This was in preparation to go to various colleges/ universities in Britain. We travelled to see the country-side and we just loved it, though it was getting a bit colder by the day. We were cautioned not to make too much noise while we were in the dining hall. All these restrictions made us feel bad, especially those of us from the third world.

At Bristol at last

Wesley Theological College was to be our home for the coming year. We were given a flat in a newly built complex named after a famous British clergy Frances Greeves. We also found a South African couple who had joined the college earlier. The man was of Indian descent but married to a white South African female. They had to leave South Africa to go and marry in Britain for it was then taboo for mixed marriages in SA.

Our joy was short lived when I came back from the university one afternoon. Wesley College was only the place we stayed in. One would cross the city to go to the university. I was a student of Bristol University. When I arrived at our flat I got news that the whole toilet system had blocked in the block of flats we occupied with some other 27 families. To my horror, it was being suggested that the couples from Africa, especially us, were responsible for the blockage because we did not know how to use toilets. I just could not believe this accusation. It was uncalled for and I did not take it lightly. Fortunately, no official came to talk to us about that and this left us demoralised. Why us? We were even smarter than some of the families, I would later find out.

The first few weeks were full of activities. We would be invited to speak to groups from the churches around Bristol. While my wife often stayed with our little kids at home, she was often patronised by some of the ladies around. They would offer to take her for shopping, for which we were very grateful. Some of the ladies would then ask silly questions like, "where her grass skirt was?" When we learnt English? And so forth. They also told her not to pick things in the supermarkets and put them in her hand bag as if we had never been to a supermarket in our own country. It was sheer ignorance on their part about what colonialism had done to us. When they saw me driving within a short space of time, they just marvelled. Little did they know that I was driving and owning a car before coming to England.

We had an occasion where we got invited to Taunton Methodist boarding school where we drove for two hours. I had the privilege to address groups of high school students. The interesting group was of those who were preparing to go to university. They were a sharp group. They asked very penetrating questions about Zimbabwe. They had done their homework. It seemed they were very inclined towards Joshua Nkomo as they did not hide their dislike of Mugabe. One student asked me if I was comfortable in my skin. Initially I did not understand the question. After thinking through it I responded calmly. I had gone around the college and seen their residences. So, I asked the student what he would do after bathing and he saw a black thing or a foreign body on his face in the mirror. The student retorted that he would just remove it off. I then told the students that I would do the same if after bathing if I see a white thing on my face. I would just pluck it off and by this I will be demonstrating that I love my skin. They also asked me if I was prepared to go back home after enjoying good life in the UK and my answer was; simple: 'home sweet home,' and they all burst in laughter.

While I was a student at Bristol University I also discovered that some westerners believed that Africans were inferior to them. I saw that a black student, such as myself, who had been brought up through missionary efforts, found themselves torn apart, on the one hand they had to be grateful to the Missionaries for giving them a basis, while on the other hand they had to spell out the truth from their point of view. One day I wrote a letter to the Editor of a regular magazine which was known as the *Methodist Recorder* and the replies by some ex-missionaries showed that they were still arrogant. In this regard, they hated those students whole revealed the truth about Africa. Some missionaries preferred a situation whereby those who were receiving grants from them had to keep quiet and simply show their gratitude. However, I am one of those people who believe in telling the truth. I cannot, and I shall not keep quiet whenever I see that there is something wrong or amiss about any situation. Below is the letter that I wrote to the Editor and its replies. It generated an exciting and informative debate. The article was entitled **"The Missionary who must never Speak."**

From the Rev Levee T C Kadenge:

How grateful some of us are, that at times we feel we should keep quiet, lest we offend the people who have been so kind to us. The Methodist Church in Britain has given me a scholarship, through the Methodist Church in Zimbabwe, to come with my family and do postgraduate studies at Bristol University, for which we are very grateful.

After a struggle within myself about missionary activities, I have decided to speak my mind out to clear my conscience. In speaking out I will concern myself with some Methodist missionaries who have been to and those who are still in Zimbabwe. Let it be clear that my views are not necessarily those of the Methodist Church in Zimbabwe.

I understand that there is a tradition here that when missionaries, both ministers and lay, come back to this country they are asked to speak to Churches here on various subjects concerning either the people or the Churches in the country in which they have worked. What a brilliant idea!

Well, they can talk about their journeys and their personal feelings, but when it comes to issues concerning the people of that country many them do not qualify to speak. I am appalled at the ignorance of the Methodist people here about the lives of the peoples whom missionaries have served. In most cases what these patient audiences have been told are the old stories of the 'dark continent' and the 'heathens' of the Third World. Such stories are very far from the present truth.

These missionaries may be entitled to speak their minds out on any issue, but let it be clear that they cannot speak for the people of the country concerned. How can one speak about the people whose language one has not made the effort to learn, whose culture one has not attempted to understand, and above all whom one looks down upon?

The kind of missionary that I am talking about has never attempted to go to the African traditional ceremonies nor tried to learn the local language. All our traditional gatherings are 'taboo' to him/her. Those missionaries who happen to attend African Sunday Services do so because they have no choice. If they attend, and they are serious, they should learn the language to understand what is being preached about.

What happens is that the missionary clergy only attend those services they are preaching at. They are rarely preached to. When one missionary visits a town where there is an English congregation, the missionary, who happens to be English and oversees that congregation, often asks this 'poor' visiting colleague to preach. Listening is one of those tools the Christian ministry cannot dispense with without killing the mission work. How can one listen if he does not know the language?

It is true that there are always locals who understand the missionary's language – English – but do all Church members trust the 'interpreters' enough to tell all their troubles or feelings to the ministers without feeling betrayed? I am not saying that one should be fluent, although this is desirable. People appreciate any attempt to learn, and it is through that attempt that one learns. Missionaries who have been to Zimbabwe for less than three years may be excused from the above criticisms because they needed enough time to adjust to the new situation.

When I left ministerial training college in 1981 I was stationed in a rural circuit in Matabeleland (Nata Circuit). I am Shona speaking and I had never attempted to learn SiNdebele, the language spoken there before. But here I was, among people who speak a completely different language from mine. The nature of the security situation in this part of our country made it even worse for me and my family. People did not trust us because we were Shona among the Ndebele.

The station had had no resident Minister for several years before we went there. To make matters worse the people I was working among use SiNdebele as the medium of instruction in schools and in conducting their services; but at home most of the majority speak another language – SiKalanga. I had no option but to learn both languages at once.

Yes, it was demanding and difficult. I had to do things considered odd to learn both the languages and the customs of the people. I had to stop using my car to use buses. This helped me to familiarize with the sounds of the languages at close range when people are free to discuss openly. In this way I was always listening, although not fully understanding what was being said.

I also went to the people's fields. I attended the people's traditional ceremonies. I also arranged with the local elders to take me occasionally to the places where they grazed their cattle. I even spent time in the bush learning the people's language.

Unfortunately, I was only in this station for two and a half years, after which I was asked to come and study here in England. During the last six months we were there I really enjoyed my work. I could now discuss any issue with the people in their own local languages. I conducted my last two Leaders Meetings without an interpreter. One thing which I did not do, despite the encouragement from the local people, was to preach in their language. My argument was that I could make mistakes and I was not confident that I could make a success of it. My wife, however, grasped the languages faster because of the nature of her work – nursing. This goes to show that one learns if one makes the attempt to do so.

There are, however, missionaries who have not only attempted but who have succeeded in learning the people's language and culture. To mention all of them will munch space. I would like to mention just a few exceptional ones who have done what most of us will never accomplish in a lifetime's work.

The Rev John White, who came to our country in the early 1900s, became known as 'Baba' White (Father White). He mastered the Shona language and culture and he was so well known that our grandfathers arrived at their deathbeds with vivid memories of that wonderful man of God. There was also the Rev H. H. M Wright, who knows more Shona riddles and proverbs than most of the present-day Shona. When he speaks in Shona, he is so clear and articulate. He retired long ago, but still lives in Zimbabwe.

I now come to the ministers still in active ministry and I pick out the Rev Brian Dann, presently at Norwich, who astonished me when he preached in Shona without a script. I still remember all what he preached before he left in the early 1970s. Mr Dann does not know me, but I just happen to have attended his service.

The list of lay missionaries can be endless, too. I will mention only here three of them. Sister Gwen Marsh, who is now retired, Sister Joan Stockley and Irene Mackay (Mrs Cooper). These were so fluent that they even were given Shona totems. Sister Joan is still in active work in Zimbabwe and is very fluent in SiNdebele and even has a SiNdebele totem.

To conclude this list let me mention two children who actually 'made it'. Deborah and Andrew Mellor. Deborah who was 8 or 9 at the time (1977) interpreted for her parents. These two children were going to a local African primary school at the mission. On one occasion these two children 'saved' the mission during the time of the liberation war. On that day the freedom fighters had come to destroy the mission and to kill the missionaries. On their arrival, they went to the principal's house, Mr Mellor was. They were received by these two children who asked if they could make them some tea in Shona. The fighters put their guns down and marvelled at the discussions they had in Shona with these white children. That is how Kwenda Mission was saved.

When I return to Zimbabwe I will speak to the people there about my experiences as a missionary in Britain. I consider myself 'a missionary' to this country whether I am asked to preach or not, to speak or not. As far as I see it now this country needs missionaries more than any other country.

When I am asked to speak to people in my country about British life and Church life, I will do so with confidence. I have been here for nearly five months now and I have so far missed one Sunday service only. In all these services I have been preached to. I have attended some of your traditional meetings, including the Guy Fwakes celebrations, the eighteenth and twenty-first birth day parties which are not different from the initiation ceremonies of some African tribes. I have gone to your pubs where people soak themselves in beer. I have also gone to the areas where the poor live, both white and black.

I live in a college where students come from different parts of this country. This helps me to have a wider perspective of this country. What I want to know is: What makes the British people tick? When I go back I will tell my people what I have seen and heard which also includes my judgment of course. I know enough English to express myself and to understand much, if not all, of what is said. If there are words that I do not understand I can always go to the dictionaries to search for meanings.

I hope that missionaries who come to Zimbabwe from Britain next will make a similar effort to learn and understand Zimbabweans their languages and cultures. Unless you look to us with same respect and willingness to learn and receive, we cannot be equal partners in the service of God.

I do not intend to discourage missionaries but to challenge them; at least to make them aware of what is expected of them. This will help us to improve our relationships as Christians and as established Churches. How can we improve race relations if Christians do not take the initiative of understanding other people? - Levee T. C Kadenge, Flat 22, Frances Greeves House, Wesley College – Henbury.)

Below I also give you the response to the above letter that I got. It was a response that was full of bitterness on the part of the writer. The writer was of those people who erroneously believed that those on the receiving end should just keep quiet and show their gratitude that way. The article was entitled **"Remembering the Pioneers"** and was from one M W Tredidgo.

"I write to express my astonishment and dismay at the letter from the Rev Levee Kadenge (14 March). A partial explanation, but no excuse, may be his youth, but during his ministerial training did he never learn of the work of Methodism and Methodist missionaries in the Southern district?

I cannot speak from the personal knowledge of the pioneer missionaries in that district, but would think that, in addition to the Rev John White whom I did know, such honoured servants of God as Messrs Shimmin, Avon Walton, and Baker, and others, were proficient in a vernacular. But when I arrived at Tegwani Institution in 1929, which was then in the Nata circuit, I served under the Rev Herbert Carter whose fluency in Sindebele was equal to that of any African in the circuit, and his knowledge of his people and their needs was unbounded. The Rev G H B Sketchley, then in Bulawayo circuit, spoke Sindebele, and later, the Rev Forshaw was fluent in that language. When he was transferred to Mashonaland he had enough knowledge of that language to get by, as did Mr Carter during his chairmanship.

These missionaries, as will all who served during that period, were required to pay regular visits to Kraal schools when they camped at the schools and met and talked with their members. Those stationed in Mashonaland spoke a vernacular and knew and served their people.

I would remind Mr Kadenge of other women missionaries in addition to those he mentions, who were fluent in vernaculars and knew the people they served – Muriel Pratten, Marjorie Baker, Hannah Thomlinson. But these were before his time.

Another matter that Mr Kadenge does not seem to realize, but must understand, is that as Africans were trained for the ministry, and standards of education and training improved, it was obviously better for these to minister to their own people, and this arrangement increased. Who could serve African people better than an African pastor? Not even a European, however knowledgeable and devoted. Therefore, missionaries from Britain had less need to be involved as pastors to Africans and exercised a more specialized service.

Next, I must refute the jibe that missionary delegations tell their hearers the 'old stories of the dark continent.' I did hear such sermons 70 years ago, and if the missionary was from China we heard of the cruel practice of binding baby girls' feet; such stories were then true. Today, OSM services are very different.

Finally, Mr Kadenge does not indicate in any way the present situation in Zimbabwe. In what were once known as 'English circuits' the congregations now include a good proportion of African members, and African ministers are stationed in these circuits and serve with acceptance, although as with European ministers some are better than others! I hear from correspondents of valuable and inspiring services conducted by these men.

I sincerely hope that after all the advantages and benefits that Mr Kadenge is enjoying, he may have served his Church and people and earn the reward that came to such predecessors as Matthew Rusike, Thompson Samkange and Simon Chihota. – W M Tregidgo, 225 Hawthorn Road, Bognor Regis, West Sussex. (Tuesday, March 28, 1985).

I immediately replied the article. My reply was entitled **'Freedom of Speech'.**

"I was not astonished or dismayed when I saw Mr W M Tregidgo's response (March 28 – "Remembering the Pioneers") to my letter of March 14.

He suggests that my youth might be a 'partial explanation, but no excuse' for my ignorance. Should I wait until I am older? Should I wait for someone to tell me when to speak and what to say? I thought in this country there was freedom of speech; so, I took the opportunity and privilege of speaking.

Mr Tregidgo is entitled to his own opinion but that does not invalidate mine. I sympathize with Mr Tredidgo's concern that I mentioned some missionaries and left out others who he thought I ought to have mentioned. I had many private responses that I expressed the same concern and suggested some few names I should have included. I agree I was wrong to have mentioned names. *However, the missionaries that I mentioned by name in my previous letter were by way of examples. I did not intend a comprehensive list.*

As far as my ignorance of Methodist missionary history in Zimbabwe is concerned, the subject matter of my present dissertation at Bristol University is directly concerned with the role of missionaries, particularly Methodist ones, in Southern Rhodesia/Zimbabwe. I am very much aware of the history of the Methodist missionary involvement in our country before and after independence.

I intend to write a book on such missionary involvement in our country and will include in it a comprehensive list of missionaries that Mr Tredidgo and others have mentioned. I will, however, make my own assessment and offer an independent interpretation.

I do not fully agree with Mr Tregidgo when he asks – 'Who can serve African people better than an African pastor?' We have had some European ministers who have served us better than some African pastors. What is important in ministry is not so much that one has expert knowledge or specialized training in anything, but that one is **with** *the people.*

Sending one to language schools does not in itself guarantee that one is going to be 'with' the people. The technicalities of the language can be learned in such a school, but it is in the natural setting of the community that the language is properly understood, and it becomes a window into the local culture. Without the local language – I insist, one cannot understand the people or enter their world. Above all, it is the ATTITUDE of missionaries that is crucial to their ministry.

I do not want to comment on the so-called 'English circuits' situation which Mr Tregidgo proudly describes lest I cause unnecessary conflict at home in Zimbabwe. My primary concern and final plea on this subject is that attitudes must change.

*Most letters I have received congratulate me for the courage to write the letter I wrote to the **Methodist Recorder**. What I fail to understand is why it should take courage to speak the 'truth' in a Christian community? Who or what should one be afraid of? Is not the authority in Church derived from the truth of the Gospel? Or is there a crisis of authority within the Church. Secondly, surely if one believes in the risen and powerful Lord Jesus Christ one is not afraid to speak out; or is there a crisis of faith as well?*

It seems that the Church both local and abroad has a crisis of authority and a crisis of faith. It is time we sought God's guidance and not the opinions of 'experts' within the Church. – (Levee T C Kadenge, Flat 22, Frances Greeves House, Wesley College, Henbury Road, West-bury-on-Trym, Bristol.)

These correspondences are very important in my life. First, this was the beginning of my writing career. It was through these letters that I realized that I have a vast potential to write and communicate with the wider world. These letters gave me the impetus to continue writing since then. Right now, I have published more than 300 articles in both local and international newspapers and local and international journals.

Second, I have learned that we should be free to express ourselves. The truth will always be true, and no one has the power to dismantle that which is true.

Since then I speak the truth. I will always speak out whenever I see it fit. No one has the power to stop me from speaking the truth. Even some dictators of this world have tried by every means to stop me from speaking but I have told them that I shall keep on speaking. I have always associated myself with those that call themselves the "voices of the voiceless". Here in Zimbabwe I have received several death threats from government security details simply because I speak on behalf of the oppressed, the suffering or the downtrodden.

CHAPTER TEN

LOCAL PREACHING IN BRISTOL CIRCUIT

As a Methodist preacher I would be placed in a circuit wherever I went. The period I was in Bristol I was a preacher in Bristol circuit. The circuit had several stations around the city. I was also invited to the nearby and not so nearby circuits in Wales. I remember going as far as Pont pool, deep in Wales one Sunday. I preached to a mainly elderly congregation. One member took me aside after the service and confided in me that the only problem they had was their minister who was only 48 years old. They were all over 70. And worse off, the minister was a woman.

My children were 'mobbed' by the few children who had come to Sunday school. Most the white kids had never seen a black child at close range, so they were all over their heads touching the hair. One young boy came to me and was touching my skin. He thought that I had 'faked' by painting it with charcoal. He was really convinced that I was one of the coal miners who had come back. The mine had just closed, and he used to see miners looking like me. To his amazement the 'coal' did not rub off.

After completing my Post Graduate Diploma in June 1985 at Bristol, I was contemplating going back home when message came from London saying they had secured a place for me to do my Masters in Scotland. It was felt Scotland was more welcoming to foreigners than England. And true to their assumption, I later discovered that Scotland was colder weather-wise but the people there had warm hearts.

Holiday in Europe

Come mid-June, we had a pleasant surprise when we were invited to go for holiday in Switzerland. We were also to attend a Moral Re-Armament Conference in Caux. This was our first trip to Europe. The snow had dried up and the weather was just superb. We enjoyed the conference very much which ended on a high note when several Zimbabweans who had attended the meeting grouped together for 'home catch-up'.

Between the meetings we had to go down to supermarkets to buy dippers for our small daughter. One day, in this huge shopping place, we failed to locate where the dippers were. We could not communicate in the local French language that the workers used. Finally, we summoned the courage to ask but to no avail because we just could not understand each other with the workers in the supermarket. We pointed to the bottom of the baby and they gave us deodorants. After some time, we hatched a plan. Since the last dipper had not yet been spoiled we took it off and brought it back into the shop. One of the helpers had her last laugh as she pointed just behind us where the dippers were stocked.

Two weeks in the Lake District

The Lake District is one of the most favoured places for Holidaying in England. A friend of ours organised that we take a break there for two weeks. He arranged with a local farmer who agreed to go on holiday as well when we were there for our break. The farmer left his farm to us. His house and everything in it belonged to us for that period. We were supposed to feed his animals, which we did with the help of a helper who would come from time to time. Most of the time, though, we were travelling in this beautiful part of England. We visited Shakespeare's original home and other small towns in that area. It was indeed very refreshing the after hard work of studying.

Some other activities that we did included going on boat trips on the lakes. We also went on train trips using old steam trains. This was much fun especially to our children. After each day of intensive travel, we went back to 'our' farm for a well-deserved night rest. The generosity of the farm owner was out of this world. We did not buy any food. He had stocked all the food one needed. We beat the cold weather by making born-fire every night. Such was the kindness of some British people.

At the end of the two weeks we had not even covered half of the Lake District area, we later learnt. But as for our part, we were very much satisfied. We left very contented a family. On the promised date of coming back the farm owner came back, and we did the hand-over-take-over ceremony. Thank God all his animals survived during our stay there.

A Well-earned British Driver's Licence

My journey to Aberdeen was memorable. I had just completed a year driving in the UK, using my Zimbabwean Driver's licence. The rule then was that after a year one had to take a British driver's licence. This meant that my licence was supposed to expire a day before I was to travel to Aberdeen. I had already done my lessons for driving and the day before we left I went for the test.

I was so composed. I was taken around by the inspector, who was very meticulous. On coming back to the VID depot, he broke the news, like, 'you can try next time.' He looked at me and I said, "That's fine I will try again." Then he laughed and said that I had passed the test. I embraced him, and he did not know why. I then broke the news to him that I was leaving Bristol first thing in the morning of the following day. He commended my driving and asked me to fill another form to get my papers done. I could have driven without their licence, but I did not want to break the law of their land. My British Driver's licence which and still have expires in 2022.

The next day we left around 3am British time. The mini cooper we had was packed with all our belongings. The luggage on top of the vehicle was bigger than the car itself. When we arrived in Aberdeen just more than 900 miles, I could not walk properly the next three days as my whole body was numb. On the way, we had been met with racist treatments which bordered on lunacy. For instance, some petrol stations refused my credit card and demanded cash on buying fuel. We did not give up and arrived around 7pm at our new place which was to be our home for the next two years. And for those two years there was no single day which passed without coming across a racist remark.

My wife was working doing all sorts of jobs to keep life to limp. I also joined her during these times I was not at school. At times I could wake up early in the morning to sweep in supermarkets and other companies to get some extra money to buy things to take home. In those two years we changed three cars and the last one we brought back home, and we were with it for the next twelve years.

Preaching in Aberdeen Circuit

Aberdeen Methodist Circuit had several preaching places along the North East coast of Scotland. I used to drive to all these places to preach whenever I was given 'appointments' which were many, though. One time I went very early to Peterhead, a new place I had not preached at before. I did not know the location of the church and I assumed that some people would help me locate it. When I asked the locals, they just could not figure out where the church was and yet it was just nearby. In Zimbabwe many people would know where any church would be. This was indeed a very strange place for me. Because I had arrived early, I decided to go to the beach. There was before Church began a man who ran towards me because he had seen me wearing a clerical collar. This man advised me to leave because it was taboo for fishermen to see a clergy man before they left for fishing. It was a bad omen because my being there would invite death. The lot of fishermen are very superstitious I was told. For their sake I left.

I was told that a lot of the fishermen were a superstitious lot, and for their sake, I did not persist but left abruptly.

Up, North there was a preaching place where the congregation complained about my accent. They said they could only hear very little because my accent was strange. I responded by also saying their accent did not even make sense to me too as well. And for sure they had a very heavy Scottish accent which was very rural to me. So, we had to learn to listen to each other carefully. By the time I left we were very much in good books. They missed me, and I also missed them too.

CHAPTER ELEVEN

A VISIT FROM MY MOTHER

One day in 1986 I had a special visit from my mother albeit in a dream. My mother had died in June 1981 just before I graduated from UTC. When she appeared in the dream, my mother was very much in agony. She had died of cancer and her last days were very painful. This was not the first time my mother had visited me in dreams after she had died but, on this day, she had a special message for me. Each time she visited me she would be bringing a message. When she came as happy as she always was it meant there was good news for me. Those times when she appeared while in agony, like she did this time around, I knew something bad was going to happen. She did not give me time to either greet her or to ask what was wrong. I told my wife early that morning that I was going to receive bad news that day.

I left for my university office. Masters students had the privilege of sharing offices. I shared with a student from Japan. My spirits were down that day and my friend noticed my strange behaviour and became very inquisitive, which made things worse.

Around 9am, a phone call came through and my friend picked it up. It was from the Chaplaincy Department. The caller just wanted to know if I was in. A few minutes later the chaplain came in and invited me to his office. On the way, I began to relive my dream and was convinced that something bad had happened. For a while, he was just beating about the bush and then later he broke the bad news: that my sister-in-law who was staying on my stand at home had been struck by lighting that morning. We were two hours behind Zimbabwean time, time-wise.

Some folks at home rushed to the nearby primary school and phoned straight to the university. Strangely enough, I was the first person to hear about the sad news. I communicated with our London Church Office and the same night I was on the plane going back home.

My brother had not paid *lobola* and the in-laws were just firm that we pay the lobola before burial was done. Seven heads of cattle were rounded up and it was only after they had been put in a lorry which was hired from Harare that we could start the burial. We were tossed left right and centre by our in-laws. In our culture, there is no way one can dispense of one's in-laws more-so when one had not paid any *lobola*. The in-laws just rule over the occasion and one must bow to their demands. To make matters worse in my case I was coming from the UK and they thought I had much money to give them.

A visit from my Mother-in-law

My wife was working hard and was at some point quite stressed. One day I decided to surprise her. I shared with her the possibility of her mother coming over. We were not sure whether she would agree or not. By then she was 71 years old. To our surprise, she needed no persuasion at all. We worked even harder to buy her a ticket. A passport was secured for her and she came. I met her in London. We spent three weeks with her and she blessed us so much by her visit. For her, it was quite a memorable trip and staying with her daughter and grandchildren was a delight. I have never seen her happier since.

The local church that we went to offered us so many incentives to take her across Scotland. Because of her visit, we went to the last part of Scotland – John O Groats. We went right inland through the Devil's Elbow, a dangerous place to navigate. The cold weather of Scotland did not dampen her happiness. Because of her presence many blacks in Aberdeen visited us just to be with her. She helped us make more friends. On her part she was happy that there were many people coming to our home.

Trip to Russia

In mid-June of 1986, our group in the Religious Studies Department at Queens College organised a trip to Russia. There were 14 of us in the group. Two of us were from Africa, myself and one guy was from Nigeria. The journey by plane to Moscow was uneventful. At the time Russians had their coldest winter in decades. Up to now they saw that it has never been that cold. We had to board a train from Moscow to Leningrad. Our Zimbabwean Ambassador to Russia was very unhelpful when I took time to visit our embassy, just to say 'hello'. I was ignored like I had come to spy on them. A courtesy call was all I needed but this was met with disdain.

The train journey to Leningrad exposed me to the harshest of weathers. The temperature was reading minus 40 degrees Celsius at the train station. We were advised not to stand still otherwise our feet were going to stick in the ice. Even with the trotting on one spot we were doing the weather was just unbearable. The warm clothes we had brought with us from the UK were nothing. We had to buy some other warm clothes for their weather. Every human being you met was, literally a chimney emitting smoke, as the cold bit on us.

Once we were on board we realised that the train was very warm inside, and the worries of the cold outside were behind us for the whole night's journey. As the journey progressed, I be-friended a young Russian man. This time I did not repeat the Switzerland mistake. I took an English-Russian dictionary. We started to converse with the young man using our dictionaries for he also had one. We had little time to sleep for we had a very interesting talk through signs and our pocket dictionaries later. He invited me to his parents' home.

A taxi came to pick me up the following morning. This is the time when Mikail Gorbachev was in power, but Russia was still a very secretive community. The family that hosted me looked after me very well. They all had dictionaries in their home for the father was a journalist. He shared with me the inside of Russian politics, and how dangerous it was not to tow, the line. That night they took me to one of the most prestigious Russian Opera house and I enjoyed myself. I had never been in an Opera house before.

Church life in Russia was by then very difficult. There were only seven Cathedrals that were open. Just imagine, millions of Russian, going to those few Orthodox Cathedrals in Leningrad! The services started very early in the morning went on for the whole day. There was no time for the ministry of the word. In one corner there would be a funeral being conducted. In the second corner there would be Communion being served. In the third corner there would be a wedding taking place. In the fourth corner there would be baptism. People just went in to 'kiss' the icons and leave for others to come in. After we had had a chance to enter the church we waited at a distance just marvelling at the stream of people flocking in and coming out with glowing faces. Just entering the place was enough.

Leaving Russia was a nightmare. Compared to our coming in our exit experience was more than hell. The two of us the blacks, were treated with much disdain. I was stripped of my clothes like my Nigerian friend. There were three people in this cubicle who were interrogating me. They searched in every part of the body and I just wondered what they were looking for. Our plane was delayed by thirty minutes. I will never forget that experience. Later, in my life I had a similar experience, in Israel, but the Russia one was a cut above the later.

The African Pastor in me

Though the University had a very viable Chaplaincy Department, at times they had to come to people like me whenever they were faced with pastoral situations concerning students from Africa. One day one Kenyan Anglican priest by the name Kariyuki just woke up mad one day. He was spotted walking in town in his morning gowns. He had to be restrained by some drugs. When I was approached by the chaplain he was at a loss. He did not know what to do. He referred me to the Church of Scotland which had sponsored the Kenyan priest to study at Aberdeen University. The church was ready to be advised and the only advice I gave to them was to arrange for his wife to come to Aberdeen. We did not tell him.

The church in Kenya worked frantically and within a week is time the wife arrived when I took Kariyuki to the airport he thought we were sending him back to Kenya. Upon seeing his wife, he became very normal and that was the end of the story. Kariyuki was so attached to his family that this 'imposed' separation ate into him to the extent that he lost his mind.

The fourteen students who were in professor Andrew Walls' class were all from abroad. The largest number was from Africa. We were students at the Centre for the Study of Christianity in the non-Western World. Professor Walls was an Africanist par-excellence. He had been a missionary to Cameroon, Ghana and Nigeria but he had also travelled extensively across Africa.

One day we got news that he was not well and had been admitted in Glasgow University Hospital for a major operation. We decide to pray and fast for his well-being and we did so. When he came back he took time before he came to our class. When he came at last he broke sad news to us that he was only given six months to live by his doctor. He was so excited that the Queen Mother paid him a visit and wished him well when she was passing through Glasgow. Prof Walls was given Member of the British Empire MBE among other honours given to him.

We regrouped and prayed and thanked God for bringing him back to college. Meantime he was always telling us that he would finish marking our theses before the six months which, he was given to live were up. He was just close to 50 years of age by then. However, he is still alive to today as I write.

Another disturbing experience we had as students of Prof Walls was when one of our lady lecturers had a funeral in her family. Her mother had died, and we were informed informally. We decided not to go for her lectures for we thought she was still mourning her mother for she was not yet buried. She looked for us but could not find us and she was very angry with us. We told her that we could not just come because in our cultures it would be taboo to go to work while your mother is dead and not yet buried. She told us that she was not very close to her mother, so it did not matter. We insisted it mattered, to us, least so we refused to attend her lectures until her mother was buried the following day.

One day I came across an advert in the local newspaper paper advertising a type writer. I desperately needed one, so I phoned the number that was in the advert. A very old voice answered the phone. I explained to the old lady who answered that I was from Africa in case her neighbours were worried about my presence because she was also blind. When I arrived and told her that I was a Minister of Religion, she was so excited that she kept me in her house for over an hour. She confessed that she had never seen her pastor for the past twenty years. She was in her late 80s and looked frail but very clear in mind. After giving her money for the type writer she asked me to stay a little bit longer.

Somebody phoned, and she picked up the phone but the person on the other side put the phone down and then she swore to herself. I asked her why. She then narrated her story. It was her son who was checking whether she was still home, or she had been taken in into a Home. She then confided in me that what her son did not know was that she had changed her will and the house was going to a charity organisation Society for the Propagation of Christian Knowledge SPCK.

The previous week before she had fallen into the freezer and had her hands stuck in it for a while until a helper came to rescue her. Besides her, there were many old people who would die in solitary only to be discovered by some milk men upon finding out that the milk they were bringing was not being taken. They, in turn, would report to the authorities who would destroy the doors to find out that the occupant would have died some days ago. Service providers are now picking the pieces. This shocked me to the core. I discovered that the several millions of Britons who live to very ripe ages of over 80 years are ignored by their children and relatives to die very unpleasant deaths. Each one is minding their own business. The best they sometimes do is to put them into Old Peoples' Homes. I have, nevertheless, heard of some horrendous stories about how some of those in these Homes are sometimes treated badly. I ask, which way, Developed World?

Further Studies

After completing my Master's, Degree in Theology, I decided to enrol for a Doctoral study with Edinburgh University, about 250 miles away. My sponsors agreed that I was not going to leave Aberdeen. I was then commuting on a train once every week to Edinburgh on Mondays and coming back on Fridays. I was staying in a bed and breakfast place which became my second home for the whole of 1987. I enrolled as a non-graduating PH. D student. This meant that I was only registered for one year. The idea was that after that year I would then come back home and enrol with the university of Zimbabwe. My stay in the UK was not supposed to go over and I complied with Church regulations and left the UK in December 1987.

Rare Hospitality

Three times in our journey in life three families left their homes for us. The first was in the Lake District in United Kingdom in 1985. A farmer went on holiday and left his entire home and farm to us. He stocked all that was necessary for us to look after ourselves for the two weeks we spent in the Lake District. My wife and our two children had the freedom of the home.

The second time was when we were on our way back to Zimbabwe in 1987. We drove from Aberdeen to London. On the way friends arranged that we would stop over near Manchester for three days. They arranged with a family we had never met before that we would stay with them. To our surprise after our arrival they abandoned their main bedroom for us. They went somewhere and left us to our own devices.

The third time was when my wife visited me in 1991 when I was in Scotland for six months doing research work. A young white lady abandoned her flat to us for the three weeks my wife visited me. She also stocked her pantry with what we needed to survive on. Such was the warmth of hospitality we experienced in UK. Of course, there were many families who stayed with us while they were still in their homes. They offered us their spare bedrooms. While we have had the privilege of such welcome we are afraid we have not done much to others.

CHAPTER TWELVE

BACK IN CIRCUIT WORK IN ZIMBABWE

Before I left the United Kingdom, I had made some arrangements that a South African of Indian origin comes to Zimbabwe as a missionary. The UK Methodist church obliged, and we came together to Zimbabwe, at the end of 1987. I had never seen an Indian Christian in Zimbabwe, so I felt strongly that the church in Zimbabwe would benefit from being exposed to him and his family. The Rev Dr Emanuel Jacob was stationed as a lecturer at UTC while I was stationed as Chaplain at Sandringham High school being the Superintendent of Chivero circuit at the same time.

This was the most difficult experience we had when the church embarked on changing the system of running our schools. We were transiting from the missionary era when they were in complete charge of the schools. The missionary on the station was both the Principal and the minister in most cases. Where the white principal was a layperson, there would be a missionary who was the Minister. When the missionaries were leaving, the Headmasters assumed the roles of overseeing the schools. The African priest was only concerned with church work. There were instances where there would be a white Principal and a black Minister. The Minister's role was basically chaplaincy work and had nothing to do with the running of the school. The District chairman had an overall responsibility because the school was in his/her district.

By the time I arrived at Sandringham the idea to change the way we ran our schools had already been muted. Naturally there was a lot of resistance. By the time we had most of our secondary schools being run by African Headmasters or Principals. Most of us ministers were not very qualified to do both as the missionaries did. The Headmasters were comfortable with running the schools without the involvement of ministers. The President of the Church then, who was himself a former teacher, was convinced that the church should run its schools with the direct involvement of the minister stationed at the school.

A lot of misunderstanding arose in most of our schools as a result. Sandringham was the worst affected. It also depended on the minister who was there. There were some ministers who were comfortable with the status quo, with the Headmaster being fully in charge. The Government's Ministry of Education was playing what appeared to be double standards. It would announce that schools belonged to the churches and they would be as run per Church Regulations. At the same time some Ministry officials would give more powers to the Headmasters. If a minister at a school felt he or she could have more stake in the running of the school, the push to do so was more pronounced. I was one of those who decided to take the bull by its horns.

Hell broke loose at Sandringham. At one time there was a strike by pupils that left the house of the Headmaster destroyed. Obviously, the blame was put on me directly. Nevertheless, there were some elements within the school who took advantage of the fluid situation and played politics with the students. Therefore, whatever then happened some of us could not escape the blame depending on who was listening to who at a given time. But the Head of the Church was determined to see this change taking place, the Headmaster had to leave the school. It was not an easy task though. The Ministry of Education played double standards in a big way. Relationships between the Heads and the Church administrators just became sour by the day.

This became the order of the day in most of the Methodist Church in Zimbabwe seven high schools. If the Head of the Church had not been involved in the running of schools before, he could not have been firm. This was his familiar territory and he was convinced that things could change. A situation arose where the church was being taken to courts by some Headmasters. At last the Headmaster at Sandringham left having put up nasty fight. Looking back, that was a very unpleasant experience, for relationships were strained in a very big way.

Most of our clergy who were not in schools at that time failed to comprehend what was happening. They sided with the Headmasters who, most of the times were so kind to them when it came to the way their children who were in these schools were treated. Before a Policy framework on helping the children of ministers was put in place some headmasters went out of their way to accommodate children of a few ministers. In some instances, they got away without paying fees at all. Because the situation was now changing from that direction some of the clergy who were in schools became isolated, for the gaps were being closed.

I for one became very unpopular. Headmasters were only trying to help minsters who would not pay fees at the end of the day. Morally it was a bit unfair. It was only after a policy was put in place clearly stating that made clear that ministers' children would pay a third of fees that the situation improved. There were some ministers who took much offence on the changing system.

As I write now the situation has changed dramatically in all our schools. The Minister who, some few years ago, were Ministers in Charge, are now Principals by designation in our schools. The journey was long and painful and some of us paid heavily. The qualifications of our ministers have improved too so they are acceptable by the school staff. In fact, we have now a Policy in place that ministers to be stationed in schools should have a first degree at least. Some of our Ministers now have degrees in Education. There is a much-improved toleration rate for each other across the board.

Circuit Work

As Circuit Superintendent of Chivero circuit I had fourteen stations to look after. All the church meetings were presided over by the Superintendent, a toll order indeed. Besides taking services at the high school, I also preached quite intensively in the surrounding churches. The furthest society in the rural community was some 24km away, at Marirangwe South. On the pastoral front it was also a nightmare. I ended up doing very little in that direction. What I concentrated on was to train the local leadership to look after the affairs of their congregations. I even went further to teach them to conduct burial services on their own. Leaders were very happy by being empowered in that direction. We also had one congregation in Norton town which was about 34km away. Norton is in the opposite direction while other societies are in another area. It was an isolated station because there was no other station in between. The only way for Norton society to grow was to put resources there so that a minister could be stationed. At that time the resources were scanty, and nothing could be done to help Norton grow. The minister went there once in a quarter, that is in three months. There was no hope for Norton to grow.

CHAPTER THIRTEEN

FORMATION OF ECUMENICAL SUPPORT SERVICES ESS

Upon my return from the UK, in 1987 I met my long-time friend Jonah Gokova with whom we had formed Buriro/Esizeni/Threshing Place Theological Institute. Jonah had done theological training at Cliff College in Britain. He was not keen to join the pastoral ministry, but he was very much involved in theological issues. At that time, he was working for the Lutheran World Federation as Programs' Officer. His Department was called ESS.

When the department was being phased out seven of us from different churches decided to come together and continue with some aspects of it in our own new way. It took time to come up with what we wanted to do. We were a group of like-minded people who felt we had much to offer to our Churches and to the community more than what the Churches expected from us. We put our heads together so that we could spend the extra energy we had by putting it to good use.

We were all agreed that protocols and demands and limitations put on us by our churches were difficult to break. Hence coming up with ESS which was going to act independently to further the work of God was the only way we would subvert the frustrations met in churches which are so rigid often.

Jonah became the Co-ordinator and I was the Vice Chairperson to Rev Bvudzijena a Lutheran pastor for a couple of years. Later I became its Chairperson.

We conducted a few workshops across the country. We even went into the region. Because of our versatility we gave birth to several other organisations like PADARE/ENKHUNDLENI/MEN'S FORUM on Gender which is now a stand-alone Non-Government Organisation. We also gave birth to Zimbabwe Coalition on Debt ZIMCOD, an organisation which dealt with debt issues. It is also now a separate NGO. The other product of ours was the Zimbabwe National Pastors Conference ZNPC. This group became the mainstay of ESS for a very long time. All these products were given birth while I was the Chairperson of ESS.

A Manyika Appreciation

One election time in the 1990s I was assigned by the Zimbabwe Council of Churches to supervise the monitoring of elections in Manicaland in the Eastern Highlands of Zimbabwe. I travelled extensively in the district. On my trip to Nyanga in the same district I decided to pay a courtesy call on my sister Emily (Mrs Nyakudzi) who was teaching at Nyafaru High School with her husband. I did not know the place where teaching.

I drove to Troubeck Inn the last place I had been to in Nyanga area. Beyond that it was a virgin land to me. As I was contemplating what to do next I saw a man by the road side. This man who was flagging cars down many of which just passed him. While the majority did not stop others stopped and he talked with the drivers, but they also left him there. I then approached him and asked him how to get to Nyafaru. To my surprise he said that was where he was also going.

We had a wonderful journey together. He was showing me the beautiful places along the way. He became my guide right to Nyafaru. His dropping place was just less than half a kilometre from where I was to turn to the high school. As he was about to leave the car he asked how much he was going to pay for the ride. He could not believe it when I responded that it was me who was supposed to pay him for his consultancy work which he did. His response was "Munombori SaAni?" meaning 'who are you'? I answered, "I am SaKadenge." People in Manicaland use the prefix Sa which is interpreted as either to mean Sir or 'child of'. This could either mean whose child, are you or just a title Sir.

Manyika people are known of anglicising everything. They talk of skuru (school) rather than chikoro as other Shona dialects use for the word school. SaKadenge is not what we say in Zezuru dialect, but we use vaKadenge. I did use the former just to be in tandem with the Manyika people. We parted very happy people. I have always told this incident repeatedly. Indeed, that man could not believe his fortune to be driven for such a long distance without being asked to pay a large sum of money. Hiking in Zimbabwe is not necessarily free. I normally do not give lifts to people but when I do I do not ask for money. I take advantage of these rides and share as much as I can with my passengers and in most cases I get a lot from them in terms of information and knowledge.

Ph.D. Student

As soon as I arrived back in Zimbabwe, in 1987 I started the process to enrol with the University of Zimbabwe UZ for my doctoral studies. I was shocked to discover that all my efforts that I made at Edinburgh to start research were not considered by the UZ. The practise at the UZ was that any prospective student should have a good pass at Masters, level, which I had, but further, one had to write a Proposal first before being enrolled. The proposal would be a well-researched paper of about 30 or more pages. You had to present your research to the Department of Classics and Religious Studies. It took me three years to come up with an acceptable proposal. By the way I was a part-time student. Though the UZ system is cumbersome at the end by the time the proposal is accepted, you will already be an expert in your area of research.

The University engaged me as a Tutorial Assistant in 1990. At that same time my proposal was accepted. I went to the university and spent the days there researching and conducting tutorials which were in my area of study African Traditional Religion. As most researchers often do, I also 'abused' my students by giving them assignments which were in my area of study; "death and mourning". Because the students came from all over Zimbabwe, I had an opportunity to have a very wide perspective of African culture and practices about to death and mourning. I did, however, finally acknowledged the vital contribution my tutorial students made to my thesis.

Besides getting some extra cash, it helped me in my research work. I had decided to study African culture as it related to Christian practices. The specific topic had to do with "Death and Mourning". I was convinced that once I know this area I am home and dry. Our people become themselves when death visits them. In Mhondoro area, especially in Chivero the people there became 'my research area.' I became an honorary member of the local Traditional Dance group at Chikowore. This became a window into the surrounding community. Chikowore was just about 7km away Sandringham where I stayed. The late Rev Z. Watyoka a Headmaster by profession was a Local Minister, according to our Methodist Church tradition and was at the same time the Headmaster of Chikowore Primary School, for several years. His wife who was also a teacher at the same school, was also a member of the dance group.

The turn-over of Supervisors was bad at the UZ that made my research work very difficult. At the beginning of each year I got a new Supervisor. It was like we were starting afresh again every time. The university, however, understood my plight, more-so the Department. We had to break all the rules of finishing a degree after a designated time. I finally graduated in 1998 after a very long study period. I had had five Supervisors in succession.

Prophet-cum Traditional Healer Camps in the Mission

Life in Mission Stations is full of surprises at times. I woke up one day to be informed that the mission had been invaded by a 'Prophetess'. He Church in Africa the church has produced its own prophets. These are men and women, boys and girls who imitate the Biblical prophets. They prophesy, heal and pray for the sick. Some do it for free while others do it for a fee. They use all sorts of things, as instruments of healing, which range from the use of oil, some milk, broilers, stones and water to name a few. The 'prophetess' who came to Chivero used milk, oil and broilers. She hailed from Chipinge, an area to the East of Zimbabwe, known for such healers. From this area also come popular traditional healers and various medicines of both good and bad.

I had heard similar stories about these 'prophets' coming from afar. While many people talked ill about them, however, a few people sought help from them clandestinely. The church did not condone such acts for they caused divisions in communities. Now it was in the mission itself. There was no way we could ignore this. The ball was in my court. In my case there was room for me to ignore it for I was only left with seven days before I was to be moved to another appointment. I was with a choice either to deal with the problem or leave it to my successor, the Rev John Jabangwe. After careful consideration I decided to take the bull by the horn.

The church's practice is that when such an issue arises, the Superintendent Minister calls a Leaders' meeting and it will be up to the meeting to discuss the problem and agree on what action to take. Discussing with tenants on the farm, everyone was against both the practice and the presence of the healer.

To my surprise when I called the meeting on a Friday no one was prepared to talk in the presence of the family that was hosting the prophetess. I was leaving the following Thursday. The couple was a very respected religious family. The husband was now a retired Evangelist and the wife was a 'bloused' Ruwadzano/Manyano member and a Local Preacher of great fame. overall, they were a feared couple. Also, many stories were said about their nefarious activities, but I did not want to believe the people.

The healer's patients came from both the mission and surrounding community from which most of the circuit membership come from. Those from outside the mission just wondered how such a person could be accommodated in the mission. In the meeting I tried to persuade people to talk but to no avail. The meeting was being help in the church. The couple sate by the entrance of the church, the husband on the right and the woman on the left. After a while of persuading the people to talk I stood up and broke the ice by saying it as it was.

First, it was first the man who stood up and walked towards me, cursing and shouting, calling me a junior in the ministry and all sorts of insults. The woman followed, in, a frenzy, coming to the front table where I was sitting literally. The two had a 'field day' of making noise and saying all sorts of profane things. The woman finally got hold of her dress and wanted to remove her clothes. The people started talking and advised that no one should restrain her. They felt that if they tried to refrain her she would go ahead and take off her clothes. But when no one came near her she began to calm down.

In that frenzy, but now no longer holding her dress, she went for my Bible. She picked it up opened a few pages from the end and with much force, tore the bible into two pieces. She threw it to the ground. After that, she went into the middle of the room but close to me and said,

"You are like an egg in my palm". She said that, demonstrating as if she had one in her hands. "I have the freedom to pull off my hand and its finished." The demonstration got even more pronounced.

I never moved an inch as she was making all those gyrations. I then pronounced judgement and said that the woman had been removed from church membership forthwith for a period to be determined later. She would not be allowed to put on her uniform until she goes through a renewal process at the guidance of the church.

She emphatically rejected my judgement and the couple left in a heft. One by one we left the church in disbelief.

The following morning some clouds just started gathering in the sky. Suddenly there were rains when much of the sky was clear. One bolt of thunder struck so close for our comfort. I retorted that it was so close. Electricity went off and there was smell in the house. Both the refrigerator and the four-plate stove were burnt. When I looked at the back of the stove where the smoke was coming from I discovered that the electric wires were burning. We thought it was the usual thunder but very close indeed.

A few minutes later, one retired Evangelist, Mr Machida, came through our home on his way to the bus stop. As he approached our house he saw something strange at the back of the house. He called us out and showed us that one of the big trees behind our house had been struck by the bolt of lightning. The tree had had a deep cut that separated two branches. There was a sign of dark smoke showing clearing along the tall tree. People in the community were just waiting to hear where the lightening had struck only to hear that it had struck at the minister's place.

It was only the previous night that I had been threatened by the couple that we 'disciplined' at the Church. It could have been coincidence but that did not worry me very much for we were still alive. Message went into the village that the minister had missed death by a whisker. I did not take a hoot about that. Indeed, I was scared when the bolt struck, but a few minutes later I had all the confidence that whatever had been intended for, did not work out.

An hour later some neighbours started flocking to our house for word had gone around. I was expecting people to come for prayers to thank God for His protection on us. Those who came first started suggesting that I go to a traditional healer who is an expert in removing the sting of thunder all to my surprise. In local tradition, there is a strong belief that once some lightning strikes, it leaves *mazai* (eggs) or 'a sting'. If these are not removed it will come and strike again. So, these diviners are called in immediately to remove the *mazai* (eggs). I refused to take that advice and instead asked for prayers.

Come Thursday a lorry came to pick us up to our next station United Theological College, having left a cloud hanging over Chivero. One Wednesday I had my final meeting with Chivero farm's tenants. I was the chairperson by the virtue of my being the Superintendent minister. The tenants pleaded with me to join them as a tenant. I told them frankly that Chivero Mission would be the last place of choice for me to live in. This was not the first time they had pleaded with me to secure a plot in the mission.

By Christmas of 1990 we arrived at United Theological College. I had spent three eventful years at Chivero (1987-1990). No regrets at all. I refused to be intimidated by any situation. I was very confident my successor was going to inherit a situation which was with one lesser disciplinary case. The community of Chivero had a lot to learn from how we handled very difficult cases. As far as I knew the lightening episode was closed without consulting any diviner. The tree has carried the bolt scar for a very long time now. The Lord protected my family and the community in a very special way during the trying times we were in Chivero Circuit. I forgave that woman who tore my Bible. It was a gift given my wife by the College (UTC) at my graduation. My wife also forgave the woman. She even came to see us off.

A special Gift from Chivero Circuit

It is often the practice that when a minister is leaving a station, a farewell party is organised for him/her. Our send-off service was organised at Chikowore church at the end of 1989. Chikowore was a bit central, considering the other stations in the country side.

The day was well organised. We were showered with gifts which ranged from kitchen utensils and clothes of various shapes and sizes. To crown it all, we were given some hard cash amounting to $67.00 (Zimbabwean dollars). By that time this amount could buy a cow. I took the money straight to my home and bought a heifer and named it 'Chivero' in remembrance and honour of the gifts received.

Ten years later, in 1999, there were 10 cows from Chivero. After four years, 'Chivero' was competing with its first offspring to give birth to other cows hence that big figure by those days. At the same point, I could tell that the cows had become too many for my relatives who were looking after the cattle. I then decided to dispose of them. I gave away three and slaughtered two for meat.

To dispose of the last five, I invited my brother-in-law and his mother my mother-in-law to come and visit us. In our culture, sons-in law, pay *lobola* which includes several cattle. In my case I had been left to pay the last five cattle. I brought them home and surprised them by taking them to the cattle pen to show them what was due to them.

They were so thankful. Since they had nowhere to take the cows to, they invited bidders to come and buy them. By late afternoon they had all been bought.

I remember my brother-in-law telling me that they were leaving by lifts to town. Perhaps, because of excitement he had forgotten that I had brought them in my car. I drove them back to Harare with all their cash. Indeed, they were a happy lot. I was also very happy that I had fulfilled my responsibility as a son-in-law. Very few sons-in-law finish paying lobola. In some cases, grand-children remain paying lobola for their grand-fathers. I thank God I managed to do it in good time. But from that day onwards I had no cattle and no home to call my own. The hut that I had built in my father's home only remain as my cherished property in our village.

CHAPTER FOURTEEN

LECTURER AT UNITED THEOLOGICAL COLLEGE

I had taught both in Primary and Secondary schools, before but lecturing was another task worth learning. I learnt on the job and soon I started enjoying it. By middle of year, I had to go back to the UK for 6 months to do research work on my thesis. I was based at Edinburgh university. This was the time the church in Aberdeen organised that my wife joins me for three weeks. A young Scottish nurse abandoned her house for us. She bought what was necessary for sustaining us for that period. I was amazed by such love and to this day I wish if I could do the same to someone else.

Back at UTC for one year I was the Chaplain to the students and then the following year I was appointed Vice Principal. All these posts had challenges of their own. On top of that, I was the representative of my Church at the College. This time most of the current senior ministers in our church passed through the college. Most them were single students. Several them had problems related to their journey to settle into establishing their own families. For example, the late Bishop Zebedia Pfebeni who was a few years younger than me, although he was single, became very handy in mediating on some of the petty and even serious misunderstandings that arose because of the growing pains that were rampant in that period. He would come to my office on his own and then would say, jokingly, "Sonny, these young people need your guidance. If you shut them out they will get more confused. Take it easy Sonny." I was his lecturer, though, but he would go such far to cool matters down because there were times when I could have taken matters to higher offices. Because of his efforts, many of our current senior ministers survived the chop from College.

Forgiven but not Forget

What I have learnt in my long life dealing with students is that one must be very careful how one relates with them. Never talk about another teacher or another student with one of them. That very day the person you talked about will know it. It maybe a little bit later but they will know at the end. On one incident, one student wrote an anonymous letter to the Head Office asking for my removal from the College. He stated a number of allegations and finally asked, 'Is he the only one who qualifics to teach here? Please save us by removing this man. He has become too big for his shoes.'

I tried to find out who did it. For a fact he/she was from our church. I looked at the assignments matching the writing to several them. I shortlisted four, then two and finally one. When I called the student at my house and showed him a page of his assignment without revealing his name he agreed it was his writing. I then showed him part of the letter without revealing his name or revealing to him that was the letter he had written. He agreed that it was his hand-writing. When I then showed him the letter he quickly owned up that he had written the letter. He said he was representing a group of 7 students who had ganged up to write the letter. When pressed to say who they were, he then turned around and said he did it on his own.

The student apologised. I consulted with Pfebeni and he advised me to forgive the student as usual. I went to the Head Office and told them that I had found the student who did it. The Head of the Church asked me what I wanted done to the student. I said since he had apologised and that it did not take time for him to accept responsibility, I was prepared to forgive him. I forgave the student. I put this incident in my memoirs to demonstrate what I have always argued about a statement many Christians say as if it is Biblical, 'forgive and forget'. Forgiving someone is not an easy thing to do. Pretending that one has forgotten is not also true. It is like equating 'forgetting' as a virtue. I often say forgetting is a sin. It is a disease. The moment I start forgetting my name something has gone wrong. Should then someone dare pray that they forget.

Christ should have said when he forgave those who nailed him on the cross that we should forget the incident. Instead he said when he gave the Last Supper to the disciples that they should always remember him by partaking in the Communion he served at the end of the meal. We do remember the meal and the Supper each time we partake of the Communion. For me carrying the cross means to forgive while you remember what happened. In the case above I should have forgotten that a student during my stint at UTC in the 90s wrote an anonymous letter. I still remember his name, Rev Amon Chidongwe, but I have forgiven him.

What will my grand-children say, suppose someone bit my finger off before they were born and when they ask me who removed my finger and then I say to them because I am a Christian I no longer remember them because I forgave them long time ago? They would say I was a stupid old man wouldn't they! Maybe, you will continue to meet this person in life but while you remember him/her you should always continue to pray for them. For me that is true forgiveness. We need not pretend that we have forgotten unless we reach the 'age of dementia' and that is a medical condition which might come naturally but which no one should apply for by praying that we may forget. Remembering, for me, is part of carrying the cross daily. Christ said, "take the cross and follow me." Christianity is not cheap grace. It took a cross to be of help. And for Christianity to make any sense, the cross must be carried daily.

Visit to Israel

In October 1993, I had an opportunity to accompany some students to Israel. The Rev Dr *Shumba* Lowe, a Germany national who was then one of our lecturers at UTC organised yearly trips to Israel for the period he was there. This time he asked me to join him going with the students. He was not very clear when we were planning the trip to the extent that I did not fully understand what he meant when he was saying that he was taking me so that I would be helping him. At the airport in Israel, he handed me some keys of a car. Thank God I had taken both my British and Zimbabwean driver's licences with me.

Hell, broke loose when I discovered that in Israel they drive on the right side of the road. Lowe was driving a twelve-seater van and he gave me a small Uno Fiat with three students. For the next 13 days we drove just over 3600km across the length and breadth of Israel. We went as far as the Golan Heights both in Israel and Syria. As I write, there is fighting in Syria and this reminds me of the sights we saw in the northern parts of Syria.

We also went to both the East and West Bank of Palestine. A few highlights included us floating in the Dead Sea, washing at the place where Jesus was baptised, a visit to the Upper room in Jerusalem, the Jewish wailing wall, a visit to both the Mosque and the Temple, the tomb of Moses, the Holy Sepulchre, the birth place of Jesus in Bethlehem, the time we spent in the Ki boots, Mt Olives, the via Dolorosa way, the tombs of Jesus, walking on the Masada and passing through various check points.

For me Israel proved to be the most security conscious nation I have ever come across. The experience I had in Russia became a picnic in the park. At the airport our group saw hell. I had a brief case which had the initials ND and the security at the airport wanted me to tell them the full names denoted by those letters. I had only bought the brief case a few days before we started our journey in Harare. To make matters worse it was a second-hand thing which I bought in a second-hand shop. They were adamant that if I failed to give them the full names I would be put on the next flight back home. Dr Lowe did a lot of diplomatic negotiations and we finally were let in. On our way back, the plane had to be delayed because a suitcase was suspected to be unaccompanied. After a long delay they later discovered that there was no such a thing and we finally left.

A Confession

In 1994 two of my brightest students at UTC qualified to further their studies at the University of Zimbabwe. They were Simbarashe Sithole and Jimmy Dube. They were offered places at the university to continue with BA honours studies. This opportunity would be withdrawn if they were to postpone their studies. It was Church Policy that students do not proceed with studies until after serving the circuits for two or more years and only after they were ordained. The university was very clear that once they do not take the offer they would not be given the same preference. I took the students to our Head Office to explain this.

In the office of the Head of the Church, I was literally dressed down in front of my students. When we were asked to leave the office I politely asked the students to leave first so that I would talk to the Head of the church alone. However, I was told to go together with them. With my tail between my legs, so to speak, I also left and there was no further discussion because I was told that was not negotiable. I was numb to tell the truth. It was only when I left the office that I became angry.

I took the students into my car and we drove back to college. The same day I gave both students some money to go to their rural homes in Zvishavane and Esigodini respectively, so that their forms would be filled in by their parents for them to access university grants. After coming back, I gave them, the permission to study but not to tell anyone.

They proceeded with their studies and did very well. One of them went on ahead to do study for a Masters, Degree in Islamic studies. The other went to the States and proceeded to do two Masters, Degrees and a Doctorate. One was our immediate past Presiding Bishop, and the other one is the current Dean of studies at UTC. He is now the General Secretary of the MCZ as I write. The other is now serving as superintendent in All Souls circuit.

All this I had forgotten, only to be reminded by the other one how I used to push them to go for studies, yet they had been officially refused. I am very grateful to these two because they did not let me down. There were a few who went for studies officially but did not come back in time and others were later 'disciplined' for one or two things and the church would have lost a lot of resources in training them.

CHAPTER FIFTEEN

CHAIRPERSON OF EDICESA

Since my arrival at United Theological College, I was invited by the Zimbabwe Council of Churches (ZCC) to sit on the board of a regional publishing organisation called Ecumenical Documentation and Information Centre for Eastern and Southern Africa (EDICESA). By that time ZCC had discovered my writing skills and sitting on that board was the best further training I was offered by the Council. In 1992 I was elected to be its Chairperson for a 6-year period. EDICESA covered some 13 countries in the region of the Eastern and Southern Africa. These covered Mozambique, Swaziland, Lesotho, South Africa, Angola, Democratic republic of Congo (DRC), Malawi, Zambia, Kenya, Tanzania, Uganda, Namibia and Zimbabwe. For those years I travelled to each country it represented. EDICESA had been established by the Fellowship of Councils of Churches in Southern Africa (FOCCISA), of which ZCC was part.

EDICESA was established to supply information from the Christian communities on Apartheid South Africa. Apart from holding workshops and seminars we published magazines and books which were a result of some of the workshops we held. We were also involved in organising groups of church leaders to observe and monitor elections in the region.

The most memorable election monitoring exercise I did was the 1995 Mozambican land mark elections which ended the fighting between Renamo and Frelimo. Another unforgettable yet gruesome election was that of South Africa in 1994 where several thousands of people were killed. Witnessing these elections and many more across the region exposed me to the cruelty which was so barbaric.

The conditions in Mozambique made me contract 'synopsis' a disease of the nostrils. I slept in a hotel room with a fan turned on for the whole night to chase away mosquitoes. From that day on, I could not breath properly for the next six years. I had to use some nasal drops to clear my noses every 3 hours or else they just could be blocked. It proved to be very expensive to buy the drug.

Little did I know that I was going to be addicted to the drug. I could put the drug in my nostrils just before I went into the pulpit. I had to shorten my sermons or else I could end up with closed nostrils. Since that time, I learnt to deliver very short sermons. Preaching did excite my body and the medication did not last long, an hour was enough before I took some.

It was only in 2001 when I was Adjunct Lecturer at UTC when I was invited to preach during the Wednesday early morning Communion service that a miracle happened. I was preaching on the text that talks about when Jesus had been invited to go and cure the daughter of the Centurion. On the way he passed through healing the woman who had been flowing blood for twelve years.

During the sermon I could feel myself being healed. I had ignored taking my medication before I climbed the pulpit. After the sermon I just did not use the medication from that day. The problem I had with my nostrils disappeared completely while I was preaching. A miracle had happened on my body. I thank God for the miracle. Hallelujah!

1995 WSCF Centennial Celebrations

The World Student Christian Federation (WSCF) was established in 1895 by the likes of J.R. Mott and others. By 1995 the movement had completed 100 years of existence. The world-wide movement celebrated its centennial in style in Berlin, Germany. I was one of the 100 lucky few who assembled in Berlin for this memorable occasion. I had joined the Student Christian Movement in Rhodesia in 1971 when I was doing Form IV at St Mary's near Harare. And later re-joined the movement when I was a student at UTC. I rose in the movement from leadership at branch and national levels. After my student days I automatically became a Senior Friend (SF).

Student Christian Movement of Zimbabwe (SCMZ) has shaped me in my Christian journey. It's a student movement which encouraged students to be more creative, questioning and being practical in the application of their faith. It encouraged debate and consultation and acting. It helped me to think outside the box. Since I joined SCM I have never been the same person in my life again. In the final analysis I give credit to this movement for giving me the confidence in my Christian faith.

During the celebrations in Germany we were invited by the mayor of Berlin and had lunch with him on the river Ryne. It was a memorable event in our lives. The whole world was represented on this grand occasion. The Senior Friends included the first black former general secretary of the World Council of Churches.

One incident I will not forget was when I arrived at the Berlin airport on my way back. My plane was in the afternoon, but I decided to leave the place where we had the celebrations in the morning. One thing that contributed to my going early was that everybody else had gone and communication was now a problem since the staff there did not speak English.

I took a train to the airport in Berlin but then I took a taxi for the last lap of the journey. I left my bag which had all the travel documents including my passport in the taxi. I was at a loss as to how to trace the taxi. Germany taxi's, at least at that time, were all yellow in colour.

Since I was early I decided to go back to the place of the Conference but not knowing exactly why I what I was going to do there. I barely made it and found the place. When I arrived, I just wondered how I was going to communicate with those people I had run away from.

I went up one floor and tried to put forward my message, albeit with much difficulty. As I was going back down the stairs, I saw this man holding my bag. It was the taxi driver. I had told him where I was staying for the celebrations. He spoke very good English. I recovered everything that was in my bag. I could not believe my fortune. I just wondered what could have happened if this could have happened in Zimbabwe. I could have lost everything in the bag. So many things were going on in my mind. I had just read in the papers that a Nigerian man had been put in jail because he was found without papers. He was believed to have been be peddling in drugs. I thought such was going to happen to me if I had lost my identity documents. The taxi man became my 'angel of hope.'

I boarded my plane a very happy man back to Harare in one piece. Later, I wrote a letter to the Herald showing my gratitude to the German people.

Fired from UTC

Coming back from one of my several trips abroad in December 1996 and this time coming back from Mozambique, I landed at the Harare Airport around 6pm. By 9pm I was already in bed because I was very tired. Unfortunately, we had a phone line in the bedroom. Around 9.30pm the phone rang, and I grabbed the phone which was besides the bed. It was the voice of my Head of Church. He said, "Tomorrow a lorry is coming to pick you at 9am." I quickly asked, "Why bring a lorry? I can jump on the taxi and come to the office." Then he went ahead to break the news I never expected. I had been moved from UTC and at no notice at all. I tried to ask why, and I was told that it was something we were going to discuss later after I had moved.

At 9am the lorry was waiting outside our house at UTC. We started packing and by 1pm an 8 tonne, lorry was full and heavy with load. By 3pm we were back at Chivero, back to that woman who had promised to kill me. When I pleaded with the Head of the Church to spare me Chivero he did not brook that. But there were more than a hundred other stations I could have been sent to, I thought in my mind.

All along some problems had arisen at UTC which had been brewing for some time. The situation became so tense that the College Council had to intervene. A meeting was held before the day I came back from Mozambique. It was resolved that the Principal was to be removed on the condition that Kadenge also gets transferred too. The decision was made when my Head of Church was not there. He was unable to attend the meeting. He was only told the decision of the College Council.

I was confused. I was just wondering what was going on in my family. My wife was working at Athol Evans Hospital and all my children were at Widdecombe local Primary school. We had to manage all those transfers instantly. The situation was indescribable. Such was how the church treated us.

Some friends came to our help with all sorts of ideas. One idea was to seek the help of the laws of the land. I had friends in the legal fraternity. Tawanda Mutasa, a very intelligent lawyer with the ZCC at that time, came in handy. Everyone was convinced that I would win the case. He drafted a letter to the late Bishop Jokomo of the United Methodist Church who was the chairperson of the College Council then. At a second thought, I intercepted the letter and decided not to take the church to court.

Looking back my abrupt removal was the best thing that was done. I sometimes just imagine if I was given a few more days to pack and how

I would have taken it. I imagine how the family could have survived during that period. Perhaps therefore a guillotine is sharp. The job must be quickly and done with. It was painful, but the chop was smart and incisive. The after effects had to be managed carefully, though. Quickly, I decided not to harbour grudges. This has always been my plus. I even joked about my being kicked from UTC with those who cared to listen. It was hoped that by playing it down I could be able to pick up the pieces, which I did.

CHAPTER SIXTEEN

BACK TO CHIVERO CIRCUIT

Being the Chaplain again at Sandringham High School and Superintendent of Chivero Circuit was not going to be a stroll in the park. But by this time, I was now a veteran of any situation. I could tell I was on top of the situation right from the start. In a sense I was coming back like a hero. Many tenants celebrated my coming back because I had proved during my previous stay that I was a no-nonsense man. Obviously, there was another group that just did not believe their misfortune. I, however, did not want people to feel down and under. I tried to reassure everybody that I had come for their good.

This time around there were different problems both in the Primary and Secondary schools. A new Junior Minister had been added to our staff in the circuit. It was a welcome development for it meant sharing of the workload. I offloaded much of my chaplaincy work to my junior Rev Cleopas Kadzere. He was working much with the primary school. Little did I know that was the mistake I made. Meanwhile he was also in charge of the mission affairs.

Sooner than expected there were accusations of witchcraft being thrown around. Both the Minister and the Primary School Headmaster had the propensity to accuse each other of witchcraft. For instance, if there was dog's waste at one's door it was believed the other had put it and it was for witchcraft purposes. At one time there was a miscarriage in one family and the other was accused of having caused it. Finally, the Minister just hired a lorry and the next thing I heard was that he had left both the station and the Ministry at the same time. What a tragic story that developed in my eyes. The blame was put on me, especially on the part of the two. Each side felt I was siding with the other! I was indeed in a dilemma. I am happy that, as I write, the Minister has been re-instated.

The Creation of Democratic Republic of Congo (DRC)

The land problem at the mission at Chivero was simmering all along. When I came back, the children of some tenants were clamouring for their own pieces of land to settle on. Church policy did not allow a 'wholesale' type of distributing land to tenants' children. The Church devised a system which would discriminate those who were not married in the church. The children did not brook that. They invaded a bush area a distance from the original village and started clearing it for settlement. They called this area DRC. This was the time when the then President of Zimbabwe, R.G. Mugabe sent his troops to Congo to fight on the side of Laurent Kabila. The reason for giving the name was multifaceted, to scare me from going there and to suggest that the place was a war zone and ungovernable.

Establishment of New Churches

For the first time, new prayer groups that were not sanctioned by the church sprang up within the mission area. Most of these were led by 'apostolic' churches. Our youths flocked to these groups. Some of them developed to be big churches. Outsiders would come to lead the churches. The church was at pains that such a development could happen on the mission. To make matters worse most of them were children of the tenants who invited and supported these new developments. We were in a quandary as to how to handle the situation. As such ZANU PF got ammunition against us. How could the Church stop other 'faiths' to worship in a Christian place? Faith healing was at the centre of the planting of these new churches.

Need to Build a manse in Norton

This was the time to develop Norton church work. We could not do it while there was no resident minister there. The Norton 'society' was so small and we did not think that it could build a manse for a new minister to live there. They were still struggling to build the Church then. I shared this with the new Headmaster at Sandringham Mr John Ngara and we muted the idea of selling the manse at the mission to the school so that the proceeds could be used to put up a manse in Norton. Since the school wanted to build a manse for the chaplain, we felt that that money could be given to the Church in exchange for the existing manse. We shared this idea with the Head Office and they quickly bought into the idea. The transfer was made, and the school officially owned the money given to the circuit. Work in Norton started, and we built a very big manse there.

I never lived in this Norton manse, but word went around that I had taken the money personally. This was very painful an experience. Moneys of the church are managed by a Treasurer together with the Circuit Steward and the Superintendent. Every transaction had to be signed for by any two of the three. In our case the Superintendent had to be one of them. Funds ran short as we were about to put the finishing touches to the manse.

Now as I write Norton is a Circuit on its own with five congregations. They are even talking of dividing the circuit into two circuits or more.

A new owner of a plot

A few months before my move to a new station I had a meeting with the Farms Committee at the mission. In that meeting calls for me to acquire a plot rose again. I brushed them off as usual. After some serious thinking I called the Committee again a few weeks before my departure. This time I surprised them. I started the meeting by telling them a story of the prodigal son. Then I dropped the bombshell and said I was the lost son. I now wanted to get a plot. The meeting was unanimous. The meeting ended quickly, and I was given a delegation to take me into one of the bushy areas to make my choice of land for a plot. I went there with one Mr B. Mugwendere who was chairperson of the Farms Committee. I identified an area and we caved thirty acres of land. Together we stood in the centre of this piece of land and Mr Mugwendere knelt to bless the land. At last I had accepted what I needed to have done long ago.

I quickly put resources together and bought some fencing wire and some treated poles and fenced off the place. I left the station when the fence was in the middle of being erected. This happened only some six months after I had given away all my cattle as reported above. I was now a proud owner of a plot in Chivero. I began to wonder how I was going to stock some cattle in my new home again.

I had no clue as to how to stock cattle on my new plot. I started regretting why I had given away all my cattle at home. It was going to be easy to ferry them to Chivero had I not given the away. Little did I know that I had done the right thing. God had great plans for me. Something must die to resurrect.

I sank a bore hole and there was just too much water. One Mr Charles Dube offered to live on my plot. He moved with his family of five. We agreed on a monthly salary and for the following months we were looking for means and ways of clearing the land and hiring cattle to till the land for us. Our first harvest was very big. We never anticipated getting three tonnes of maize. By the time of this harvest I was already settled in Highfield and was commuting back and forth to monitor the crop progress at the new home.

CHAPTER SEVENTEEN

ESS *KAIROS* WORKSHOP – HIGHFIELD CIRCUIT

Between 21-22 September 1999, the Ecumenical Support Services (ESS) decided to hold a workshop for both the clergy and laity in Harare. Highfield Circuit of the MCZ where I was serving, offered to host the workshop. The broader aim of the workshop was to afford Christian leaders in Highfield an opportunity and space to consider various challenges emerging in their area of ministry. The specific objectives of the seminar were: (a) to equip pastors and laity with analytical skills; (b) to look at strategies to fight the ills of Highfield together; (C) to strengthen the ministry of the church in Highfield and (d) to come up with solutions to the problems of Highfield.

The only guest who did not show up and to the disappointment of the local leaders was the then Member of Parliament Hon Richard Shambambeva Nyandoro. The other Speakers who made it were Dr P. Dhliwayo who tackled the subject of 'Living conditions in Highfield and their implications for health', Mrs Magaya who spoke on 'Opportunites and challenges of business in Highfield', Police Chief Inspector Mubaiwa, on 'Crime rate and its effects on society in Highfield' and Rev George S. Magamba who spoke on the 'Theological implications and challenges for Christian ministry in Highfield.'

Besides the sessions we had we also had some time to visit some areas of interest. We went on a guided tour of Highfield location. Our first port of call was Machipisa Police station, where most of the participants went into the cells for the first time. We had a moment to chat with several inmates who were there. The male cell had a total of seventeen inmates when it was just about five metres by five metres or even such area less. The Chief Inspector took time to show the participants around the Police Station.

The second place we visited was then notorious Beira Corridor, so-called, because of the vices which go on there like selling of various drugs.

The third place was Lusaka Bus Terminus just for us to appreciate the problems faced by commuters.

The last place was the pub. This place is about 400m from the manse but the then minister of the place, Rev G. Juru had never visited it, despite her having been in Highfield for nearly six years. Most participants had never been in a bar and that was their first experience.

Rev G. Juru, to her greatest amazement, met one of her members there, having a good time. The member did not wait for the Pastor to confront her but just came straight to the Pastor and confessed that the individual no longer belonged to her church but was now a Catholic. That must have been something. What amazed most of us was how patrons in the bar responded to our visit. Although some of us had clerical collars on they thought we were visitors from the City Municipality which looks after the affairs of beer halls in the city. Those who were sitting outside started complaining to us that the place was smelling and needed sprucing up.

The purpose of the visits was to have some hands-on experience of real situations that some people who are potential converts and some who are already our members experience in their daily lives. At the cells, we met a family with food for a member of one of the ministers who was attending the seminar. They were waiting with food for a member of their family who had been arrested. Such life experiences are not reported to the Church in many cases. Indeed, the visits were an eye opener.

This was their 'Kairos challenge', as the Main Theme of the Seminar was. *Kairos*, 'meaning the moment of truth.' At the workshop, we were challenged that as messengers of God we must tell the people the truth. Jesus came as a liberator of the oppressed and the captives; *"The Spirit of the Lord is upon me because he has anointed me to bring good news to the poor. He has sent me to proclaim release to the captives and recovery of sight to the blind, to let the oppressed go free, to proclaim the year of the Lord's favour,"* Luke 4 v 18-20.

Impressions of the tour of Highfield

Participants at the workshop observed that the Police Camp was too small. They were surprised that its toilets were inside, and they were flushed from outside by the police or someone they assigned. They did not see any tissue papers anywhere. The cells were dark and very small for the numbers, particularly the men's. Women were only two in their cell.

The cells were smelling and there were very few blankets considering the number of the inmates. Inmates slept on the floor. The participants also observed that one of the Police Officers was not respectful to inmates whom he made to reveal their cases. Also, food was not enough. The Officers admitted that some of the food comes from their homes at meal times.

The delegates, however, agreed on the fact that the conditions were made so tough to discourage inmates to come again. They also observed that cells were very dark with little light coming through small holes on the meshed wire which was also very high. Inmates came out once a day for 30 minutes and that was the time they did exercises. The cooking utensil were very small hence inmates were brought food from their homes to supplement.

On the visit to Zororo a place along the 'Beira corridor' delegates were shocked to discover that drugs were being sold in the open in that area. The real 'Beira' is in Mozambique, but this place is given this name because there was a time when goods which were traded with other countries came through Beira and the soldiers had at some point to guard the way between Mutare Border Post and Beira, during the war in that country. So, it became the corridor to keep much needed trade going on. Youths were seen wondering about, waiting for customers. It was very easy for them to commit crimes. Here also were the homes of a few church members belonging to different denominations.

The good news about Zororo was that there were few cases of house breaking or related thefts. The reason we were told was that there was much solidarity among the residents particularly those involved in various vices. Since there was a lot of activity in the area, thieves did not get opportunities to steal. Those who stole other people's properties would rather go and still elsewhere, leaving their own place unscathed.

In the beer hall that we visited we observed that 'bad' language and 'bad' jokes were the order of the day. As Ministers and laity, we had met our church members and some who had left church before. Most of the patrons just enjoyed company and their beer. The benches were uncomfortable, and patrons were drinking from the same mug. However, this was being discouraged because of the many infectious diseases. Some in the beer hall mistook the Pastors for Municipality Officials, so they wanted to air their grievances as mentioned above. They complained about the dirty conditions, dirty toilets and yet they were buying lots of beer. They wanted conditions improved for them.

At the end of the seminar we agreed that the church should not divorce itself from its own society. The church exists for the community and not for itself. The church business is to empower itself so that it goes back to the community and minister there. For that reason, ministers should be equipped with analytical tools so that they remain relevant even in changing times. Unfortunately, we discovered that churches seemed to exist for themselves.

CHAPTER EIGHTEEN

IN HIGHFIELDS CIRCUIT

In December 1999 I transferred to Highfield Circuit in Harare where I had been appointed to be the superintendent. For the first time, I had one job in a circuit. The circuit was big, covering some five large townships. There were three of us on the circuit staff, myself, Rev M Chisvo and Rev Masvotore who were both my juniors. Masvotore and myself were new while Chisvo was there before us. We worked together very well. I had replaced the then Superintendent the late Revds J.J Juru and his wife Rev G. Juru, now retired. They had been in Highfield for 6 years. Rev J.J Juru affectionately known as 'JJ' was a hard-working minister. His workload was covering 10 townships before he divided the circuit to what I inherited. One just wonders how he did it and by that time they were only two of them himself and his wife, before Rev Chisvo joined them.

'JJ' emphasised on giving to improve the work of God. In the process, he trampled on so many people's toes, especially men at Glen View society. This society had the largest number of men in the whole Methodist Connexion. They came to church in big numbers but were reluctant to give to the work of God. 'JJ' challenged that. By the time he was leaving things were just bad. The men had refused even to contribute anything to the church.

I remember my first meeting, after he had gone, where members of the Quarterly meeting were often referring to how bad things were and how nice it was to have a new minister in my person. To their surprise, I did not take those remarks kindly. I corrected them by saying that talking about another minister with me was just like talking about me. What will stop them from doing the same when I was also gone! I really took them to task.

Some six months later, they came to me to ask me to ask me to accompany them to Gweru where 'JJ' had been stationed. They wanted to go and apologise as a group. I could not just believe what they were saying. I had not deviated from JJ's teaching about supporting God's work. I even went further to introduce the concept of tithing with me leading by example. I gave them my full blessings to travel to Gweru. I refused to go with them for the simple reason that I did not want to shield them. They had to face 'JJ' on their own.

They hired two Commuter Omnibuses and thirty of them went and spent an overnight, worshipping and praising God with the Juru family. When they came back, they were totally changed people. Highfield circuit has never been the same again after that incident.

A Surprise Gift

After just a few weeks in Highfield, I went through the records of the church and discovered that the preacher by the name of one Mrs Mhiripiri had not been 'planned' to preach. I asked the leadership, and no one knew the person except the name. I was then referred to senior members of the church who had been leaders several years before. I was given the address where she lived and was told that she had stopped coming to Church a long time ago.

Upon visiting the address, that I was given I saw this 90+ year old woman. She lived on her own. Her house was very smart, though. She did the cleaning herself. She was very sharp in mind and could tell the origin and growth of Highfield Church from scratch. She had joined preaching in the '40s and had been preaching until the '80s when she stopped going to church because of old age. Therefore, she could not be 'struck off' from the Preaching Plan. It was old age which stopped her from coming. Therefore, twenty years she had not been going to church and she claimed that no minister had visited her since she stopped coming to Church, even though some veteran leaders disputed that.

We immediately struck a friendship. She was a very good orator. From the time I met her, I did not spend a week without visiting her. Each time I got to her place, she had something new to share with me. The strange thing, though, was that I never saw any other person at her house. The gate was always locked but just after a knock she would open it.

I learnt that she had four living children three of them ladies who lived in Zimbabwe, and a son who had gone to America some thirty-five years ago but had never came back. She communicated with him by phone, quite often. But when she was not well, the son phoned almost every day. One day he phoned when I was in the house and he was told that I was there. He talked to me and thanked me for visiting and having time to chat with his mother.

About three months later she passed on. It was then that I saw a few her relatives, including the daughters and grand and great grandchildren. The funeral arrangements were suspended until the son came back. The body was kept at a parlour for the next few weeks. Sadly, the son had no travel documents and had to put everything in order first for him to come. It took almost a month before he came. When he came, people were notified, and the funeral arrangements started with the mourning wake at her house in the Engineering Section of Highfield. The son came with his American wife. They stayed at Miekles hotel in town for the period they were in Zimbabwe for the funeral.

On the day of burial, the son approached me at the graveyard and he asked me to meet him at the late woman's house for lunch with the other mourners, as is the normal practice.

From the graveyard he went straight to his hotel and came back to Highfield, having changed his clothes. We arrived at the same time as he pulled his car in and I was also driving in. He called me to his car and gave me Zim$14 000. During these years Zimbabwean dollars were a strong currency.

He jokingly said I should buy my wife and myself clothes. He went on to explain how he arrived at the decision of giving me that money. He said that when he was preparing to come home, some friends who had heard that he was coming back to mourn his mother came to help him. One couple offered to buy him and his wife the tickets to come to Zimbabwe. They had already bought their tickets when they were given the money. He said he 'heard' God saying to him, 'Go and give the pastor who was visiting your mother ten percent of the money you have been given.' So, the money I was given was his 'tithe.'

I was short of words because it was a lot of money and I felt I did not deserve it. I was just doing my work as a pastor to visit church members. When I told my wife about our gift from this man, she was also very happy. We sat down to discuss what we should do with the money. I told my wife that I was instructed to buy clothes for her and for myself. To my surprise my wife had other ideas. She suggested that since we had no cattle for our new plot we better use that money to buy them. I quickly bought into the idea.

I went to Chivero and bought a cow which was still with a calf, for $12 000.00. In less than a year after dispersing of the other cattle I had, I had started another herd of cattle with this one, which was almost giving birth to a calf. As I write I have more than forty herd of cattle.

Graduated with PhD at UZ

In the year 2000, I graduated at the University of Zimbabwe with a Doctoral Degree. The then President of Zimbabwe, His Excellence Robert Mugabe, spent a few seconds congratulating me as is the tradition with D.Phil. students. The reason for doing that to Doctorate graduates is that the students have always been fewer. In that year, there were only three of us from the Faculty of Arts. There was one Mr David Kaulemu, and a Mrs Martitz and myself all from the Religious Studies, Classics and Philosophy Department. The examination results had come through in 1998.

On my invitation list were Professor G. Chavhunduka who was the Guest Speaker. He brought a colleague representing the Zimbabwe National Traditional Healers Association (ZINATHA). Professor Chavhunduka was the President of ZINATHA. My Doctoral Studies were about our traditions, especially concerning death and mourning and these are experts in this regard.

Some Church members at Lusaka Methodist church where we held the graduation reception did not take kindly the presence of members of ZINATHA at a function they assumed was a church function. Even though my topic need one of such people to be Guest of Honour, it took much persuasion to make Church people accept and attend the celebrations. The Professor was just up to the occasion. When the members realised that he was an Anglican Church member some came to apologise. Members of our Churches do not want to be seen to be taking part in African traditional practices in the presence of their ministers. When the minister is not there they can tolerate and even take part.

United Nations Scholarship

Soon after my graduation, I was offered a scholarship by the United Nations to study for a Diploma in Administration with the South African Institute of Administration and Management (SIAM) in South Africa. I saw the advert in the paper and applied and was offered the opportunity. The scholarship was offered through the Zimbabwe Elections Support Network (ZESN) in conjunction with the Electoral Institute of Southern Africa (EISA) in Johannesburg.

I took a sabbatical leave from the church. As students, we were staying at Parktonian hotel in Johannesburg. It was my first time to stay in a hotel for so long. Though the food was very good it became boring at the end. We had to make do with *sadza* cooked in the street corners.

This was a 'crash program.' For seven weeks, every day, we were studying including Sundays. There were 35 of us from the Southern Africa Development Community (SADC) region. Two of us were from Zimbabwe. The program was to equip us with managerial skills in various aspects of the supervision and monitoring of elections. We also had special lectures on Monitoring in Troubled Situations. Those who wanted to be on stand-by in case they would be wanted to monitor in troubled parts of the world, either as part-time, or full time were asked to put their names down. When it was realised that I did not put my name down, I was approached by the Co-ordinator because she had realised that I had shown some rare capabilities. I told her that I was a full time Minister of Religion. But after some serious persuasion, I finally put my name for temporal calls.

Almost Fired from Highfield

While I was away from the circuit, the District Superintendent oversaw my Circuit. At the Quarterly meeting that I did not attend, the circuit 'voted' so that I should be removed from circuit. I say so because it was un-procedural for any part of the meeting to be chaired by a lay person. In our tradition as Methodists Quarterly meetings are not chaired by lay persons. The supposed chairperson of the day asked a lay person to chair the section of the meeting which dealt with the stationing of ministers.

I had spent two years, and the person who moved the motion that was so persuasive that when it came to vote it was against me. Such was the nature of meetings in Highfield Circuit.

When I came back and chaired the following Quarterly meeting the Secretary chose not to read that section of the minutes of the meeting arguing that it was not chaired by the right person. After some persuasion that part was read. When we were now taking the procedural formalities of correcting and approving of minutes, it was unanimously agreed that that section of minutes was out of order and should not be discussed. I tried to convince the meeting that we should discuss them and was ruled out of order myself. That was the end of the story. Such is what happens in our work at times. I continued another year in Highfield.

CHAPTER NINETEEN

ELECTED BISHOP OF HARARE
WEST DISTRICT

In 2002 at the Harare West District Synod held at Sandringham I was elected District bishop designate. On this day I was bathing early in the morning and a man came behind my back and patted me and said 'Bishop'. It was just before we went for the elections. I was puzzled but I did not respond. I just mumbled for I had tooth paste in my mouth. The man disappeared. Came election time in the mid-morning, I was elected the next Bishop of Harare West District, to begin Office in December 2002.

The months between May and December were a reflection period. Now I was going to be at the deeper end and at the helm of one of the biggest districts in our Conference. Having travelled twenty-five years in the ministry, I had given up dreaming for any higher post in the church. When I was elected, I became the oldest Bishop. Most of the bishops had travelled for less than ten years in the ministry, even some had barely served five years, the minimum requirement for one to qualify to be elected a Bishop.

In mid December 2002, I moved from Highfield Circuit to Mabelreign where I would be the Bishop of Harare West District for the next three years. We the MCZ are not an Episcopal church, like our sister church the United Methodist church whereby once one is a Bishop then always a Bishop. Our practise is that one goes into the office of the Bishop but when one's term is over. One leaves the Office and you is no longer a Bishop. One can only be a Former Bishop.

The first appointment is for three years. After three years, one can either proceed after another approval or one ends there. So, at the end of the day the maximum one can be Bishop is five consecutive years and leave. Later, one can come back if elected again. Many colleagues do not just want to accept our practise hence they would always refer to me to as Bishop. Now I am tired of always denying that I am still one. So, I have resigned to comment when I am referred to as Bishop. One always feels a bit uncomfortable. But I have learnt to live like that. Friends often remark, 'once a bishop always a bishop.' Not true to our tradition, though!

Harare West District was the largest district in terms of the numbers of the circuits and membership in the Zimbabwean Conference. I started when we had fourteen circuits while the next district which followed us in terms of circuits had nine circuits only. Had Church members wanted, the District could have been divided into two districts for some districts then had less than seven circuits.

Strategic meeting of the District

One day during the first weekend of January of the year 2003, we held a strategic planning seminar with Mr F Mapuranga, the District Lay President, Mr Chivanga treasurer and Rev R Mabodza the secretary. I acted both as Facilitator and Participant at the same time. We were all new in the office. This was not the best of arrangements when all the office bearers were new. The most interesting part of our seminar was when we were doing SWOT analysis. We concluded that there were more advantages than disadvantages. Our strengths seemed obvious to us. It was important to know our threats and weaknesses so that we would guard against them. We also looked at our proposed Five-Year Plan which we were going to share with the District. The day ended with much prayer and wishing each other well in the journey we had embarked on. Indeed, a strong team had been put in place. The exercise we went through was to pay dividends soon than latter.

Car Crisis

The District had no car for the Bishop. Before we came in, there had been efforts to buy one, but we ended up buying an old car which disappointed many people. I was part of the team that made those arrangements. One can justify what we did because we did not have enough funds to buy a good second-hand car for the district. The larger section of our members did not want to hear again about buying another car. I was then advised to use my car and the District would pay for repairs and fuelling the car. I categorically rejected the idea.

We did not agree on the way forward. I started using my bicycle for my pastoral routines in the vicinity. Then there were a few funerals of prominent members in the church that were taking place in the community. I would take a wooden peg, linen up my trousers and jump on to the bicycle. Whenever, I arrived at any of the funerals, roll I made it sure that I stood my bike on its stand rather than placing it on walls. Sometimes I arrived when some members of the Church were already there before me and they would be seeing this spectacle. This happened for some time.

One day when my assignment to go to Chivero and Sandringham High school came I woke up early at 5am and cycled all the way and arrived there at around 8.30am; 70km. After my duty there I returned and arrived back in Mabelreign at 3.00pm. Altogether I had covered some 140km on bicycle and was very tired. I did this twice.

Then one day my District Executive sat down with me. They asked me for how long I was going to use my bike. My reply was simple; if they did not buy a church car. We spent the greater part of that day strategizing for the purchasing of a car. We finally decided that a car should be bought. Once that idea was bought up by the Executive, then I could see light at the end of the tunnel.

Our next Synod in April endorsed the idea of buying a new car. A fund-raising committee was put in place, chaired by one Mr Freddy F. Manjengwa, and the Treasurer was one Mr Muzanenhamu. I remember the Treasurer being so excited that each time we met he would say, 'Mufundisi I can see the car.'

Meantime I got a present in the form of a book, from Mr T.G. Gidi who had gone to the UK. As title is: '*The Power of Positive Thinking*', by Norman Vincent Peale. After giving the Treasurer the book, the excitement increased. He was really on fire.

Next, I challenged members of the church in our District to tithe just for one month towards the purchasing of the car. At the end of June, we had raised enough money to buy a brand-new car from Willowvale Motor industries. As I write this is the car that was given to Harare Central District which finally came out of Harare West District two years ago. These were times of economic and political crisis in Zimbabwe by the way. By then the Government did not want to accept that we were in a crisis, nevertheless.

Introduction of Appreciation for ministers

As the economic situation was biting by the day. I as Bishop just wondered how ministers in my District were surviving with the meagre stipends we were getting. I did my survey in other churches and came up with the idea of appreciating men and women of God, once in a year, so that they could get something to see them through tough times. I had started something similar towards the support of ministers while I was in Highfield. When I first introduced it to the staff meeting, it was short down. In the MCZ, if members do not want a thing, they just push it to other committees. Since this had not been done in the circuit, it was referred to societies and I knew that was the end of the story. I called the then Circuit Steward who was one Mr H. Mhandu, who later became District Lay President twice. I asked for his opinion and he agreed that ministers were suffering. I persuaded him to write cheques for the ministers and then report to the next meeting that he had found it necessary to help in the interim.

To his and my surprise when he reported to the next meeting he was hailed for the action he took. That was how 'upkeep' started in Highfield. It later caught on the fire to other Districts and Circuits. Now it is an official Policy, and this is still done from time to time.

Just like what happens in all developments in church work, there were those who did not buy into the idea and there were always in the minority. The appreciation of ministers was accepted at District level; what followed was its acceptance at Connexional level. In his speech to Synods the then Presiding Bishop Rev Z. Mukandi had this to say to 2004 synods on a subheading entitled Appreciation Day, *"A new positive development has taken place in some of our Circuits and Districts, a thought of cushioning our ministers in the economic hardships and the escalating cost of living and the small stipends the ministers receive. Christians of a circuit would decide on a day they would come together and fundraise towards a special appreciation for the services they receive from their minister or ministers and hand some of their ministers as a token of appreciation and thanksgiving to God for His servant. No matter how small this token of appreciation would be, but we must thank God for the spirit in which the gift is raised."*

"Annual reception for minister: Some denominations make it a Policy that they receive their ministers once annually when they change station or whether they are returned at the same base as a way of thanking God for the gift of life and extension of time of service in the vineyard at the same base or as a way of welcoming a new servant of God. This creates a closer interaction between the minister and the flock."

This has since caught fire across the Connexion and ministers have benefitted as a result. The members are happy that they are looking after their ministers well. Appreciation Days have become big days of celebration and thanksgiving. Each Circuit, District chooses a convenient time for them. Now Bishops and the Presiding Bishop and the Lay President are being appreciated at the level of connexion.

How Times have Changed

During the period between 1990 and 1996, I was often invited to officiate by a Department in the Ministry of Education, Sports and Culture that dealt with State functions, normally opening the function with prayer etc. I presided over four funerals of some National Heroes that were buried at Heroes' Acre in Harare. I also presided over one Independence Celebration event at the National Sports Centre.

Little did I know that a couple of years down the line I would be haunted and smeared by the same authorities. My troubles began in 2000 when I started to assert my position on issues that I thought should not be distorted. It was when I was Chaplain at Sandringham High School that I disagreed with the notion that homosexuality was a foreign concept. I had done some research on the subject and as a Chaplain I had dealt with cases of boys who would have been involved in such acts. I would also hear the same from my colleague Chaplains that they sometimes came across such cases where boys stayed together. Above that a few clergies in the church agreed that homosexuality was part and parcel of African Culture but not that African culture permitted the practise. Boys played this game as they herded cattle. A number ended there but a few pursued this behaviour which later turned to be a gay life in some whilst others abandoned it totally.

CHAPTER TWENTY

RETURN OF MY MOTHER'S GOATS

My mother before she died had a gift of healing. She used to attend to very bad wounds of people affected by *nhuta*/cancer and they would get successfully healed. I used to see her go to the forest to cut alloys and burn them in the fire. She would then tie the barks of the alloy on the affected parts and after some days take them off and the wound would have disappeared. She was paid both in cash an1d kind.

Besides this skill, she also could make those who did not have children have them by giving them a concoction of medicines (*kuuchika*). I know of children who were born by couples that had taken a long time to conceive and they did conceive after coming to my mother for help. They also paid her in kind. Some of the couples became lifetime friends of my mother. Despite having all these skills, she tried to make them very private. It was not like there were queues of people waiting to be treated. As a result, she ended up having several goats. However, later, she would die of the stomach cancer.

But one day just before she died, all her goats just disappeared, and we never saw them. According to our tradition as a family, we were supposed to return the goats to her family. It took us a long time before we returned them. After four of my brothers had died, we finally went with the goats to Mhondoro to our late mother's brother.

We had bought four goats to replace those that had disappeared. I ferried the four goats we had bought in my station wagon Peugeot 504 from Chivhu to Mhondoro.

But I arrived at my uncle's home that night he refused to receive the goats. He accused me of just bringing the goats before he had gone to consult a diviner. He suspected that I had a hidden agenda and just told me to leave with them that same night.

On my way to Chivero, my new home, from Mhondoro I was involved in an accident. It was about 1.00am and as I was driving along a bend, I turned my head around to check the goats which were making some funny noises. My fear was that one of them might have hurt itself. At the same time the car was speeding. The car landed in a thick bush and got stuck there. Since the ground was very wet and the wheels got sank in the mud. I could not reverse it and at the same time I had hit a tree.

I left the car unattended and went to seek help from the nearby-village. It was very dark. No one dared come out at that time. As I was contemplating what to do next, I immediately heard voices. I called out, mentioning my name, my totem, my predicament and where I was coming from. I had left the car on in case I could not locate it when I came back. In this area there are so many cattle rustlers and it was very easy to be suspected of being one of them.

Two guys who were coming from a beer drinking spree came to my rescue. These are the people whom I had heard talking. I told them my story and they sympathised with me. Later, I realized that they were related to my uncle by totem and they knew him very well. They were not surprised that he had acted that way since they knew him very well. They mobilised others and we ended up being six of us. They brought picks and axes and around 3.00am we had managed to pull the car out of the mud. I proceeded with my journey and arrived in Chivero around 5.00am.

After I arrived home I notified aunt Monica my uncle's sister who is now British by citizenship. She went to England in the '60s. She comforted me and promised to come and sought out the issue. She eventually came and by the time she came the goats had multiplied. They were now eight because two of them had given birth to twins each. She, together with her elder sister Nelly (Mrs Zvomuya), who was actually the first born in their family, decided to slaughter the goats and they shared the meat with their relatives. They sold four of them.

According to our tradition, the case was solved there. Sadly, the elder sister Mrs Zvomuya is now late and uncle Mukomba is also late. Aunt Monica argued that the goats did not belong to uncle Mukomba, they belonged to them as my mother's sisters. She blamed me for having taken the goats to uncle Mukomba in the first place. He should only have been informed about the return of the goats.

Repayment of a Debt

In the late 1980s a certain man who used to work for Marondera Municipality had sold a vacant stand in a low-density township to me. When I went to start the proceedings of wanting to build on the stand, the Municipality asked me to bring the title deeds for the stand. Looking at the papers, the Council officials told me that the stand had already been sold to someone else. This man was once a Councillor and he had been given a stand together with the title deeds. However, when it was repossessed once he left the council. He later alleged that he was not informed of the new development. And for more than fourteen years we could not solve the problem. I had to pay $6000.00 to clear the debt. By that time, I could have bought six herd of cattle with that money.

All along, the man dodge me each time I tried to confront him. I knew I was not going to win the case even through the courts. He as a war veteran and he used that to scare me not to ask for my dues. Each time

I met him, unfortunately, were times during the national elections and by that time he would be armed with a pistol. I remember meeting one day him at Wedza Growth Point, where he brandished his gun at me. He told me to go to hell to get my money back.

Being told to be 'off' just like that was very much painful for me. My prayer was that the man comes back to his senses and sits down with me so that we could come to a compromise. I just wanted him to pay back what he owed me without any interest. And by that time the original amount had devalued greatly. The only time we talked for a few minutes I had suggested that he gives me some six herd of cattle as compensation and asked for six beasts, but he shrugged that off.

After I had given up on the issue I was contacted by a stranger one day. He introduced himself as the relative of that man. It took me by surprise why he was looking for me. The man told me that my debtor had gone somewhere in the country and had instructed him to ask me what I wanted so that we settle the case. It took me sometime to accept what he was talking about. I responded by saying I now need more than six herd of cattle because of the delay and because he had insulted me.

The man invited me to my debtor's newly acquired plot. I had never seen such a dilapidated farm house. It was like a ghost place. Some fire had been made right in the middle of a house that had wooden floors. When I went to the cattle pen there were only seven cattle. Initially I wanted all of them and they agreed with me. After cooling down, I then asked for only two of them. They could not believe their luck. I was shown a heifer and a bullock. The later could be slaughtered for beef. We went ahead and slaughtered it. I only took away the beef and I left everything else for the family. A few days later I came back for the heifer. I put it in the back of my truck and ferried it to my home in Chivero. I told the family that I had forgiven the man. They thanked me like I had done a great thing for them.

After some time, I was told that the man was had turned insane. He was now living in the forest and not in a foreign land as had been alleged. They had gone to diviners and the man was confronted by one diviner and was told that he had done something very wrong to someone. He pleaded with the diviner that this could have happened when he was fighting the guerrilla war fare. The diviner refused that assertion. After some probing he then told him of what he had done to me and that I was not happy. The diviner then said he should solve the issue. The diviner had told him to meet any of my demands.

After the payment was made and after the man had been told about the finality of the case, he came back to sanity from the bush. What I usually tell people when I share this story is that I could not have accepted the payment had I known that the family had consulted a diviner. When I am asked why, I often say that that would have been against my beliefs. I have always refused to be involved with diviners. My belief is that if someone knows about the wrong they have done they should own up and pay back. Our culture has all the negotiating avenues that are available rather than to be probed up by someone about a thing one knows of and then give credit to the diviner. Most diviners use the patients to probe a case and to come up with the remedy altogether together. For they are psychologists who use the divining tag to make their work authentic according to traditional requirements.

The Formation of the Zimbabwe National Pastors Conference (ZNPC)

For a time, we had been going through trying times in Zimbabwe, and some of us pastors had no platform to come together to air our views. The traditional ministers' fraternity meetings were not well organised and did not have coordination for them to be very effective. Moreover, these would be found in some places and not in others. As such in 2003 ESS organised an all stack-holders meeting where all known pastors and their associates would be invited. Around 300 pastors from all over the country met in Gweru and after three days of deliberations, ZNPC was formed.

The main reason for coming together was to share what was happening in the country where people were being beaten during elections. We realised that most pastors running most of the churches did not receive any training. There were also others whose literacy levels were very much questionable. So, this platform would act like a training ground. Pastors of all shades would rub shoulders with each other and this would be beneficial. We eventually ran workshops and training sessions where we tried to meet the needs of this varied group. The sessions became so popular that ESS was invited all over the country to run workshops and certificates were issued. For some of the Pastors, the certificates they got from us became the only qualification they had in their career. We observed that the pastors were being empowered each time we brought groups of them together. This did not endear well with the National Central intelligence agents who immediately started harassing some of the pastors across the country. Myself and the leadership of ZNPC as the initiators of the programme became targets of suspicion.

Come 2005 elections ZNPC successfully registered as an entity to also monitor the elections together with others. That move again made the state apparatus more suspicious. I was not worried because the pastors were now taking their role seriously as shepherds of the flock. No wonder our next AGM meeting held in Bulawayo was oversubscribed. There were over 600 pastors from all over the country.

In the same year, I led a group of seven pastors to South Africa (SA) for a pastoral visit to some Zimbabwean refugees. Of the estimated three million Zimbabweans who have left the country the bulk of that figure is in SA. We met the Gauteng Province Police Chief, Naidoo in Johannesburg. Because of the multiple complaints we got from the Zimbabweans there it became necessary for us to meet the police.

Zimbabweans complained that they were now being used as Automated Tailor Machines (ATMs) by the SA police.

Each time they were rounded up the police asked for bribes to release them. Police Chief Naidoo invited all his immediate subordinates in the province. They were over 40 of them and we had a very fruitful meeting. The amazing thing was how easy it was to meet with the Police Chiefs in South Africa in such a short time's notices.

We also had a meeting with the Human Rights Commission of South Africa. We lodged some of the complaints from Zimbabweans whose rights were being violated by both the police and SA system itself. Asylum-seekers were ill-treated and the process to be vetted was very cumbersome and it was centralised in Pretoria. The result of our meeting was that we were promised that more centres would be opened. The Human Rights Commissioner was very accommodative to our views and complaints.

The next port of call was the 'holding' centre for those to be deported. This place was pathetic, to say the least. Even though we had made an appointment prior to our going there, the place just looked inhabitable. Many of the inmates were Zimbabweans, although there were some from Mozambique and others form other neighbouring countries. We heard of some horrific stories narrated by the inmates. We then proceeded to see some two refugees, camps. The stories were getting nastier by each time. The conditions here were just deplorable. Families were crammed in small tents. They lived in fear of being mugged even in the camps. There was a lot of abuse of women and children. The sanitation was inhumane. Many folks we shared with told us unending stories of suffering. We ended up needing counselling ourselves.

There was a residential 'flat' in central Johannesburg where two floors were reserved for those Zimbabweans who were blind. This was the most horrific experience we had. We had time with a few them who told us of their stories, of how they ended up in SA. Begging in Zimbabwe had almost become impossible. The SA economy was still very kind to beggars and most of them even confessed that they were now able to survive despite the other challenges of being mugged. Some had families and that made their accommodation woes even worse.

The Methodist Central Church in Johannesburg was the hub of so many activities to alleviate the plight of the refugees. The minister there was very popular with refugees but unpopular with the SA authorities. The Rev Paul Verryn, the Bishop of this Church, was a very humble man who gave all to welcome the multitude of refugees in his church.

At night the place was just crammed with hundreds of thousands of people sleeping everywhere, on the stairs, in corridors, on benches and others spent the nights seated leaning on walls while trying to catch a nap for a sleep at the same time.

On our second visit after we had formed an organization called the Christian Alliance and we honoured Bishop Verryn with a shield of bravery. The occasion was graced by the refugees who had every praise they could shower on this man of God. Controversy did not spare the church and its leaders who were subsequently taken to task by the City Authorities.

We found out that a lot of people wanted to come back home but had no means to do so. We managed to negotiate for more transport to take them back to Zimbabwe. SA periodically repatriated those who volunteered to go back home. The International Organisation for Migration (IOM) took an active role in organising these trips back home, with the assistance of the SA government. But that was just a drop in the ocean. Families who were living in abject poverty were crying wanting to go back home. Some of the refugees were very sick and while others died there.

We warned the South African authorities of the impending relationship disaster if what we saw was not addressed. No wonder the later there was the xenophobic attacks in which several people were killed. When it ultimately happened, we were not surprised because we saw it going to happen and we had tried to avert that disaster by showing the Authorities that their lack of action would incite the South Africans themselves to act. When we went back after the attacks the situation was even worse. The fear that ran through the many 'make shift camps' left many with some psychological problems. Children suffered the most and many of them could not go to school.

CHAPTER TWENTY-ONE

THE FORMATION OF THE CHRISTIAN ALLIANCE (CA)

About thirteen of us were invited by a group of pastors to Matopos in Matabeleland to strategize and think through what was happening in our own country. We had invited a Zambian, Rev Japhet Ndhlovu, to come and help us to come up with an organisation that would speak prophetically on the political situation in Zimbabwe. After three days of deliberations we formed the Christian Alliance and I was chosen to be the Chairperson of the that group. I was going to be the Chairperson of that organisation for the next five years. The CA was formed after the Government's *Murabatsvina* (operation clean dirty) which left so many people homeless after their homes were destroyed by government. We were to speak on behalf of the many Christians because the mother bodies of Christian organisations were not speaking out.

Until the day we announced our coming on board the existing ecumenical mother bodies; the Catholic Bishop's Conference of Zimbabwe (CBCZ), Zimbabwe Council of Churches (ZCC), and the Evangelical Fellowship of Zimbabwe (EFZ), General Secretaries were quiet. They had not spoken out on behalf of the people when their houses were being demolished. Our activities aroused the spirit to speak in them. Later on, they were now coming on board as if to compete with us. The General Secretary of the EFZ came to us and told us that he had been to the Government's Minister of Information and had been told that we were not going anywhere. Such was our beginning. We were cornered but that did not lower our move to steer the waters.

One day there was a prayer meeting that was organized by ecumenical Churches which was organised by the churches but later on got high jacked by the government. I disapproved of that prayer meeting and I was very vocal then. On the weekend it was going to be held, I decided to go to Hurungwe visit to my sister. I took the then Bishop Rev Obey Mavuka and his wife who was bishop in that district. I had heard that he wanted to go there. We arrived very late on a Friday night. We were their guests for part of the night. Little did we know that when I left Harare the Central Intelligence Organization (CIO) were following us. In tracing our route, from Harare and they got lost somewhere when we turned to Hurungwe. They lost sight of the car after Karoi. We turned left but the Police were waiting to see us in Kariba. They thought we were going to Zambia, running away from the prayer meeting but they did not see us at Makuti turn off.

My First Arrest

One day in 2005 we were called to Bulawayo to go and address the Bishops there about our newly formed organisation, the CA. On our way to Bulawayo I carried with me the Rev Brain Mugwidi and the Bishop Magaya. Little did we know that we were being followed to Bulawayo the CIO.

We addressed a huge crowd at one of the Churches there. Several Bishops came to listen to us. After the meeting we slept in Bulawayo. On our way back to Harare, we did not know that the same people were following our car. We decided to travel slowly because the previous day we had been driving very fast and since now we were not in a hurry any more. When we arrived at Snake Park near Harare, we were removed from the line of cars we were in and were asked to park in the nearby fields. We protested but we did not win the battle. The guys who were following us surrendered us to the Police at a road block mounted there.

The Police at Harare Central Station asked us to wait for a little while. The guy who had apprehended us had a diary in his hands. For close to 30 minutes we waited until they had talked to the Police at Harare Central Police Station. I realised that there was something wrong and so I immediately sent a message to one of my Church members in Norton, who was a lawyer to come to Harare, telling her that they were taking us to Harare Central Police station. The Officer who had taken us told me not to send any messages, but I had already texted someone.

The lawyer texted the Lawyers for Human Rights who immediately started for Harare Central Police Station. It was on a Friday meaning to say that if they arrested us on that Friday we were going to sleep in the cells and only to be 'tried' on a Monday. On arrival at the Police Station, we saw the lawyers waiting for us there. The Police were very much disappointed to find that some lawyers were already there at the Station. They showed their displeasure but there was nothing they could do for whatever they were doing to us, we were now with our lawyers to protect us.

The Police went to our car and searched it and took out all our papers. They interrogated us and then told us to go home and come back on Saturday for further interrogations. But unfortunately, the Police detail left his diary in our car and when I went to the car I saw this diary. When I had dropped Bishop Magaya and Rev Mugwidi, I saw this dairy and asked them if they knew about the diary. They all denied the knowledge of the diary. Then I remembered that the arresting Officer had a diary in his hands. I opened it. When I opened the diary on the date we were arrested, lo and behold, there was all the information about us there. Thus, I confirmed that it was the Police detail's diary.

I called the lawyers and asked what I had to do with the diary of the Police man. The lawyer asked me to know what was in it and I told him all the information about my car and the details of the journeys that I had made with the car. He advised me that if I wanted that information I should, early in the morning look for photocopying services and get it photo copied and then I return the book if they ask for it. And, that is exactly what I did.

I now had the details of those who were dealing with our case and their phone numbers. Some of the information in it was of the trip that I had made to Hurungwe to my sister's place. They had put it this way that the car was noticed in Chinhoyi and Karoi but after Karoi the car disappeared. They promised their authorities that I was on 24-hour surveillances.

Harassment

One day when I was coming from a meeting in town I realized that I was being followed. The person following me asked me to drive home and park my car inside the dura-wall. I refused and waited at a garage a few meters from my home and then returned into town. I called my lawyer from the church and she arranged that I go to see a certain lawyer in town. I went there, and when she came out late at night, we decided to talk to my friend Jonah Gokova who quickly thought of an idea. I was supposed to go into hiding.

So, he arranged that I will go to a hotel and be kept there under a pseudo name for a number of days. I went to the Continental Hotel under this pseudo name for some 21 days. For all these days, I was being kept there as a Nigerian visitor. I did not leave the hotel until 21 days elapsed. I did not visit my home neither but was confined to this hotel as the Lawyers were trying to see to it that I was not harassed.

MCZ Conference in Gweru in 2006

The Annual Conference of the MCZ was in Gweru this time around. We arrived in Gweru on a Monday night. Word circulated that the State President was going to come to Gweru and he would reside, at the place we were using. The word was that a certain Minister of religion called Levee Kadenge and Rev Brain Mugwidi and his wife Rev Getrude Mugwidi were not allowed to be there on the day the President would be visiting. We were told, about it and we waited for the day to come. We complied and left the place when the day came. The Intelligence was looking at my car to see whether we had left. The car did not go anywhere. We did not use my car to travel from the Conference but wee borrowed an old car, and we used that car to leave the place of Conference. That day it was very cold, in Gweru so we left for the Methodist Centre, there in Gweru. No one knew that we had gone there. We spent the whole day there praying and studying the bible.

Meanwhile at the Conference they were being harassed that I was there because of my car still inside. They tried to say that I was not there but to no avail. In fact, when we left using the old car and waved our hands at the people who were at the gate, not knowing them and they did not know us perhaps these were the Agents we waved to. The CIO called Harare and they brought an arrest warrant for us. A helicopter left Harare with a warrant of arrest and they gave it to the Presiding Bishop. My name was called out, but I was not there at the venue. The Agents still insisted that I was there. We only came back when the State President had come and gone.

Chairing the Save Zimbabwe Campaign

As CA we started chairing the Save Zimbabwe Campaign meetings 2006. The democratic forces had their space shrinking by the day. We as Christian Alliance were asked to chair their meetings. This would mean that they could meet freely under our auspices. These Save Zimbabwe campaign meetings were very crucial because that was when all the political parties where grouped together to strategize inside the country. While we enjoyed our work, the Government Agents were also working to counter us.

One day we organised a very big meeting where we brought all the democratic forces together. The late Morgan Tsvangirai, Welshman Ncube and Arthur Mutambara who were opposition political leaders had not met for a long time. On this day 29 July 2006 we brought them together and we had this chaired the meeting. It was great news that Tsvangirai and Arthur Mutambara greeted each other on that day. The CIO were there in their numbers, monitoring the events of the meeting.

Arrested for stealing my own cattle

We were looking forward to our only daughter getting married on the last weekend on October 2006. The weeks before that we were busy making the preparations. But we did not have fuel to use to travel to Mhondoro and then to Chivhu. Our prayer was that we find this fuel to travel to these places. In Mhodoro in Chivero Mission where our new home is, we wanted to go there and make the necessary arrangements. There was need to spruce up the buildings there so that they prepare for this big event. In Chivhu that's where my elder brother is. He had to come and preside over the 'marriage' of our daughter. I had to go there in person and ask him to come and 'marry' my daughter. The two journeys would consume about 50litres of fuel, for they are about 600 kilometres in total away from Harare.

Whilst we were looking for the fuel, the Lord had other plans for us. Some people were planning that on this weekend, I must not attend a Standing Committee meeting in our church. As a result, they had arranged with the Police, who where now tracing my movements to make sure that I did not attend the meeting. They organised that they would take me on that day of the meeting to Mhodoro and then to Chivhu on the same day.

Early in the morning of that day a group of Police Officers came to our house in Mabelreign. Around 5 am they were there with two vehicles. When my daughter told me that some Policemen where, at the gate, I thought it was one Policeman who was our Church member. I had met him and saw that his mouth was dry, and I asked him if he had meal mallei and he had said he did not have any. I thought that he was the one who had come for it. Little did I know that it was a bigger group with their own agenda.

They were allowed in the house. They came to me and asked if I had taken any cattle to Chivhu. I said 'yes' I concurred because I had taken cattle to my brother there. So, they said that I was under arrest because I had stolen the cattle. They did not want me to explain anything. They were just interested in taking me to Mhondoro and then to Chivhu. They wanted to take me alone and my wife refused to be left behind. They refused but she insisted that she wanted to go also. They could not leave her. She also came with. They put us in the Santana Police vehicle. I was in the middle of who two-armed police men. She sat behind the car me. In the car, we heard that they were three police officers and in another one there were seven in plain clothes and a driver.

All together they were twelve people accompanying me to Mhondoro and Chivhu. We then took this opportunity to tell those in Mhondoro to prepare the place for the marriage and also to take word to my brother to come and 'marry' my daughter.

In Mhondoro they were very rough on us. They were given the documents that showed the cattle had been taken to Chivhu. After they harassed my worker, my wife had to tell them to prepare the place for the marriage ceremonies.

We drove just round three hundred kilometres to Chivhu area and we saw my brother there. He was confused to see all these people, but he could not locate the papers because his wife had deposited them somewhere else. It was only when they were about to leave that she arrived, and they were given the papers for the animals. I then shared with my brother about the pending marriage and left him some money to jump on the bus to come and marry my daughter. So, we had two drivers and two cars to carry my message both to Mhondoro and Chivhu. The prayer for fuel had been answered in a very big way. I was escorted to take these messages around, plus a host of body guards.

The sun was setting so we drove to the tar and then came back to Harare. The Policemen who were in charge told me that there was no case but just that they had just been instructed to keep me busy for the whole day. Around 12am we arrived in Harare, but the police were refusing to take us back home. My son brought our car and took us home. The next weekend my brother came, and my daughter was married very well. We were thankful and grateful for the assistance we had been given by the Police albeit not intentionally.

Cattle project

When all these things were happening, an idea came into my mind of sharing the cattle that I had with those who could not afford them. I gave four cattle to each family so that they look after the cattle for seven years and they return them, and I passed them on to the other family. So far, I have given to six families. Three families in Chivhu, one family in Njanja where I was born, one family in Macheke and two families in Chivero. All these families I gave them four cows each. The idea is that they would be just a 'start' for these families. These families would be benefiting from the draught power, milk and manure for their fields. After they had given the first heifer I would give them to be theirs. After seven years their cow must have had two calves. So, I leave them with three cattle and I will take the rest back. Their cattle would have multiplied. The first two families have so far returned fourteen cattle each.

CHAPTER TWENTY-TWO

WILDERNESS EXPERIENCE

When I started my three year-term in office as Bishop of Harare West District, I religiously followed our Five-Year Strategic Plan, and to my surprise, by the end of my initial three-year term, I had seen all my plans coming into fruition. There was no need for me to continue. We contemplated about this seriously and together with my wife we decided that we should go and bid farewell at the April 2006 Synod which was being held at Mazvikadei Dam. We hired somebody to bake for us a very big farewell cake. I sat down with my team and told them that we were stepping down at Synod because we thought we had accomplished our task.

Our cake was displayed on the table from the day we arrived at Synod until the end. Came election time, we were retained but I was not very convinced that that was the right thing to do.

By the end of the year the situation just changed for the worse for the country. My involvement with the Christian Alliance did not go down well with the State which pestered the leadership of the Church to dump me so that they could deal with me from outside the church. Headlines like "Bishop abuses church property" were published in news-papers. The church met to consider my case. I was called to tell my side of the story and that I did. Finally, we had to agree that I should step down.

The church was so kind with me that it allowed me to continue until April 2007 Sandringham Synod where my successor would be elected.

This guy would be acting until the following Conference in August of that year. I chaired that emotional Synod myself. The Synod was emotional to me because I was finally bidding farewell to the people I had worked with so well. Sandringham was also the place where I was elected as District Bishop. On another note, my wish not to continue had been heard. God had vindicated my wish not to continue. His answer came a year later when Rev Simon Madhiba was elected to act as the new Bishop of the District.

May 2007 and the period up to 2009 Church asked me to apply to serve in the sectors. I left my appointment as Bishop after just three years. For two years and eight months I was in the wilderness. During this period, I learnt to forgive. I built myself a home in Norton meanwhile.

In 2009, I was invited by the United Church of Canada to attend its 40th General Assembly in British Columbia as a Guest Ecumenical Partner.

Formed the Institute for Theological Reflection Today ITRT

The ITRT was formed in 2007 after I had been asked by the MCZ to step aside because of the prevailing political situation in Zimbabwe. Initially we had problems in securing places to work from. We finally got a place at ZCC Kentucky Hotel. We were offered a dilapidated house which we renovated. Just after completing the renovations we were shocked to be told one day at 8.00am that we were to leave the place by 4.00pm on the same day. We were very much devastated. The ZCC officials told us that they were put under pressure from the CIO that we should not be seen to be associated with the Institute which was run by Rev Dr Sifiso Mpofu and myself.

My involvement in Christian Alliance (CA) meant that the CIO was monitoring our activities daily. This meant that each organisation which I was associated with was being monitored as well. At one organisation they actually planted a lady who came in as an intern but meanwhile she was heading a regional office of the CIO. We did not know this. She came as someone who was coming from a college and needed placement work in our Accounts Department. We offered her attachment work for three months.

A week after we had engaged her one church leader came to our office and he met this lady. He took me aside and asked me what she was doing there and also whether I knew her very well. After spilling the beans, the lady just disappeared and never came to work again.

From Kentucky Hotel we agonised about where to go. We had bought some furniture and the whole house was full. I prayed that the Lord leads us to a place where we could be welcomed for what we were. It took a few hours before I just raised a phone call to one minister whom I was convinced would accommodate us.

The Rev Sikhala Cele of the United Congregational Church of Southern Africa in Eastlea was quick to give us some space in his church. He gave us the Sunday School Hall of his church where we put all our five desks. For the next six months, we used this facility without paying anything in rentals and other bills.

Later on, occupants of the offices at the church decided to leave and we moved into four offices. As I write we are using one big office for we temporarily scaled down with the hope that when we are free we will resume our activities on fulltime basis. Now we run the Institute on a part time-basis.

I was invited by the World Council of Churches (WCC) to talk about the crisis in Zimbabwe and other engagements for the Institute ITRT.

UK Methodist -World Church Office arranged that I make a trip to UK for the World Methodist Historical Conference held at Oxford and for other engagements for the Institute ITRT.

CHAPTER TWENTY-THREE

TWO MONTHS PILGRIMAGE TO AUSTRALIA

My struggle in the fight for democracy has not been confined to the four corners of Zimbabwe. God has been more than faithful to me. The sacrifices that I have made in the quest to emancipate my fellow countrymen have in some cases taken me to distant places. To me the gratification has not been out of the mere travel but having the opportunity to tell the Zimbabwean story to the world, but in the process, seeking ways of dealing with our crisis and inspiring the world to take charge of their destiny. I believe the fight for true democracy and equality for humanity is not unique to Zimbabwe only but is a global reality. Of all the journeys that I have had to undertake, I would want to share about my two months visit to Australia which I have christened the Australian pilgrimage.

I arrived at Sydney Airport on May 29, in 2010, with very high expectations of seeing kangaroos running across the air field but was very disappointed not to see any. My line of thought was however expected for someone who was visiting a country known for its kangaroo population. Though I am widely travelled, it was refreshing to be visiting a land this far-away place sharing our struggle for democracy in Zimbabwe. Jim Rumery and Bruce Burton welcomed me at the airport in the afternoon. I joked with them saying "I was expecting to meet kangaroos at the airport but was disappointed because they were not anywhere near to greet me." I said this just to tease them just as what often happens when foreigners come to our countries expecting to meet lions and Giraffes as soon as they arrive. Such stories of lions and other various wild animals roaming all places in Africa are so common in some quarters of the world.

But just before the touch-down of Quantas, the Australian giant plane, I filled in a declaration form and 'declared' my herbal teas I had brought with me. The Immigration Authorities demanded to see my tea as I was checking out. The official at the Customs Office confiscated my tea because it was not commercially packed. I tried to plead with her that, that was my mainstay, but she refused to budge in. The three packs of my cherished tea I had were thrown into the dust-bin. That tea was what was between me and good health for I took no pills or any other medication except my home-grown tea.

I shared my plight with my hosts as we travelled to Wollongong some 65 plus kilometres South East coast. They comforted me by saying that herbal tea was also sold in their shops. I was not amused because I had brought mine and that is what I trusted and not those from shops. Upon arrival at Bruce and Bev's home, which was going to be my home for the next 12 days I was greeted with a bush of one of my teas. Bruce and Bev have always grown Lavendah as part of their garden flowers. "Look here is my tea the Custom Officials threw into the bin."

The Lord who has always promised to provide with our daily needs had proved that He was a God of His Word. For me this was a sign of good things to come in Australia.

My first assignment the following day was being 'on air' with Nick Rhineberger of the Christian Radio Station 94.1FM. Nick was fascinated when I said that missionaries were brought by Christ to Africa and not vice versa. Christ had been to Africa before and had always been there. When he was born Herod wanted to kill him and God directed Joseph and Mary to take Christ to Africa for safe-keeping; I argued it was until after the death of Herod that God appeared again to Jesus' parents instructing them to take him back to Israel because the enemy was dead.

I got several comments after the interview from individuals who listened to the interview that day. The people I later on felt that it was refreshing to hear the other side of the story of Christ.

In the afternoon, Sharon Bird, the local Member Parliament welcomed me heartily to Australia in her office, in down town Wollongong. She presented me with an Australian Flag as a sign of good will. Of all my travels, this was the first to be given the flag of a nation I was visiting. Sharon invited me to feel welcome and free to express my opinions without and fetters. She expressed her best wishes for Zimbabwe and was confident that my country with the full support of the Australian Government would come out of the doldrums. I responded by saluting Australia for taking the initiative to support the Zimbabwean Government of National Unity (GNU) when other Western countries were taking their time to chip in.

The Bible speaks of a prophet as 'having no honour in his hometown.' While I value the true friends that I have made in Zimbabwe, it is equally true that I have made many enemies because of my stance on oppression. I, however, continue to draw inspiration from the fact that evil thrives when the good men remain silent. It was thus gratifying for me when Kiama Independent, an Australian publication, ran the following story upon my arrival in Australia. The story was published in Issue no 21 on Wednesday, May 26th, 2010. Below are few lines of the story as it came out.

One Man's plea (Published 26th May 2010, Kiama Independent, Australia) By Danielle Cetiniski (<u>Decentiski@kiamaindependent.co.au</u>).

Few are brave enough to stand up to a brutal regime, but Zimbabwe's Reverend Dr Bishop Kadenge is one of them.

The democracy advocate visited Kiama Uniting Church yesterday to share his people's plight with Kiama residents and to form a stronger connection with Australia......

Reality Check: Ethical Journalism as a virtue

While I was obviously elated to have received such positive coverage from a supposedly 'alien' media in Australian to borrow the ZANU (PF) terminology, that rare experience from a Zimbabwean of my position conjured memories of a partisan state media back home. A media that paddles falsehoods, spews hate language day in day out and does little to reprimand the wrongs that the Government of the day commits against its people. It is common to read negative and damaging stories especially if they involve the perceived enemies of ZANU (PF). The answers that came to mind left me with a bleeding heart. Where did we go wrong as a nation? It is very interesting to note that the article cited above recognized President Mugabe and Prime Minister Morgan Tsvangirai as the "two leaders" of Zimbabwe when the state media back home somehow negates that reality. What does that say of our Journalism? All They do is pander to the whims of the ZANU(PF) hardliners.

My faith and optimism, however gave me a renewed belief that despite the negatives, all hope was not lost for Zimbabwe. God in His own time will save our situation, but we are the wheels of the positive change that we want to see, and we must play a part in making that dream reality. My going to Australia was a morale booster. The Media Monitoring Project and Zimbabwe (MMPZ), in 2008, produced a document titled *"The Language of Hate Inflammatory, Intimidation and Abusive comments of Zimbabwe's 2008 elections."* The book documented the main sources of inflammatory, offensive and intimidating language that characterised Zimbabwe's 2008 election. It provided some clear documentary evidence of the origins and messengers of the "hate speech" that has so much traumatised and divided Zimbabwean Society today.

This anomaly was not only consistent with the 2008 elections but has for a long time been a cancer that has slowly destroyed the fabric of our society. What peace can we dream of with such a media? It is certainly a form of political oppression for the long -suffering Zimbabweans. How refreshing to go to a country where there is freedom of the press.

Media reform was earmarked as one of the key deliverables of the Government of National Unity upon consummation of the Global Political Agreement that was signed at its inception. It is, however, disheartening, to see that very little has been done to ascertain media reforms to date, save for a mere licensing of some publications and the appointment of a malfunctioning Media Commission whose credibility is questionable. The media must realise that it has a duty to inform, all citizens in addition to this issue of balance are a necessity in practice.

A good example of how the media can foster oppression is an excerpt from the Sunday Mail of 15 June 2008 which quoted President Mugabe as having said the following words: *"ZANU PF fought for you, for our right, land and a bright future. This legacy should not simply be vanquished by the stroke of a pen at the ballot just because I am not getting basic goods... Otherwise a simple X would have taken the country back to 1890. The Third Chimurenga can't just die because of an X. All those who died in the struggle will turn in the graves."*

The Australian experience

They say when chance and opportunity meet, success has got no option but to manifest. I can only safely say, my pilgrimage to Australia was one of the most successful and educative missions in my entire life. It is never too late to learn, and I am more that certain that the knowledge that I gained in Australia will come in handy at this prime stage of my life and I am positive that the assertion that 'with age comes wisdom' will equally apply in my life. The opportunity was nothing short of the Lord's doing.

Wollongong

Upon my arrival in Australia, at the end of the first I went to where I stayed with Bruce and Bev Burton for twelve days. Just the feeling of touching down and acclimatising during those first few days was refreshing. For the first time I stayed on the coast. I come from land locked country and so, spending twelve days on the coast was a bonus. I had wonderful hosts? All I can say is that the opportunity to share my experience with fellow Christians in Australia was prearranged in heaven and the Lord had certainly gone before me so to speak.

While in Wollongong, I had the opportunity to visit the Illawara Presbytery of the Uniting Church. The Presbytery stretches along the coast for a distance covering almost 85km. That was an eye-opening experience for me and I will forever be grateful to God for that rare opportunity. The wisdom and the calabash of ideas that I tapped from is second to none and by the time I left, I was a better person. I also addressed to the Synod of the Presbytery and thanked them for initially supporting and blessing the efforts of the Northern Illawara Uniting Church congregation which meets in Bulli. The presbytery promised to continue to support our work in Zimbabwe.

The major highlights of my stay in Wollongong was the chance to preach to the Northern Illawara Uniting Church and other congregations in town and the also lead article about my experiences that was published in the Kiama Independent of May 28. The article captured any experiences in Zimbabwe and how my travel to Australia was going to benefit the Zimbabwean cause and other humanitarian experiences that I was carrying out in Zimbabwe with the Institute of Theological Reflection Today (ITRT) and the Zimbabwe Christian Alliance.

A visit to Symbio Wild Life Sanctuary, during the week made my stay in Wollongong complete. I had the opportunity to see the kangaroo for the first time, and to touch one. The other animals I had a close contact with were the likes of the kookaburra, koala, the red kangaroo and many others. Even my communication back home changed tone. It was like now that I had seen a live kangaroo so what is more to see? Little did I know that I was just in the little corner of a vast and gigantic continent full of flora and fauna.

I also had a long conversation with Dr Kerry Enright, the Executive Secretary of the UnitingWorld of the Uniting Church of Australia, a development that somehow entrenched my faith and heightened my quest to fight for positive change in Zimbabwe. It was gratifying to have a Christian brother from that far sharing in my experiences and concurring with me on the need to fight oppression. While some Christian leaders in Zimbabwe have chosen to give a blind eye to the crisis of governance or even to join the oppressors through showering them with unwarranted praises, it was indeed uplifting to have a Christian leader with the interest of Gods people at heart. Christian leaders, just like the political authorities need to understand that they are just stewards who have a Higher Office to answer to in heaven.

Acknowledging service to the needy: Northern Illawara Uniting Church

It was in Wollongong that I also had time to know with Northern Illawara Uniting Church, has been supporting the ITRT projects in Zimbabwe like the fish project, food-packs distribution to Mhondoro and I took time to encourage them to continue supporting us. As a Christian leader, I have realised that true Christianity is not just about giving a message of hope and advocating for justice. The church needs to find practical ways of dealing with issues if it is to remain relevant. What good is there in preaching about the life hereafter to a hungry and oppressed person?

This has prompted me to run some projects that help disadvantaged communities back home and the Northern Illawara Uniting Church has been one of the most supportive groups to this cause. This has made me realise that sometimes it only takes initiative to help others and God then raises people to fulfil that dream.

The Bible speaks about how the five thousand where fed simply because there was some two fish and five loaves of bread available. It only took that small effort in availing little and visibly inadequate food for the multitudes to be fed. I firmly believe in God's *'law of multiplication'* and I have strong conviction that these communities sustaining projects will grow by the day and will help reintegrate Zimbabweans into their communities and also empower them. Most of the beneficiaries are victims of the 2008 Presidential election re-run violence and the economic decline that was being presided over by the Mugabe regime. Widows and other disadvantage people have been considered in the process.

While our government in Zimbabwe seems to have no capacity and will power to help those in need, it is surprising that they are also not comfortable with humanitarian organisations availing the much-needed aid? It's more like the case of a father who after realising that he has no means of providing for his family takes insult at every well-wisher's effort to assist his family for fear of being exposed. Such folly, for me, is even more damaging because a wise man would rather have his family well-fed, whatever the source, than have it starve out of mere pride. Another reason is that these people are so obsessed with power that they scoff at every initiative that exposes their leadership shortcomings.

Sydney

After spending some remarkable time in Wollongong, I then left for Sydney, the Australian largest city by the end of June 2010. Given my passion for learning and ideas-exchange, I had a memorable experience sharing with the Faculty and the ministerial the students at United Theological College in Sydney, which is a part of the John Sturt University. Sharing my experiences, with the students and the Faculty gave them a better understanding of the person that I am, my personal experience at the same time giving them a challenge to awaken to their social responsibilities as they carry out their ministerial duties.

It is true that ministry today calls for more than just preaching the gospel. One needs to be in touch with the realities affecting their flock, otherwise ministry becomes irrelevant. No wonder why before I left UTC (Sydney) a consignment of books and tutorials was to be posted to Zimbabwe ahead of my return all at the expense of the College in Sydney. Thanks to the principal Dr Clive Pearson for extending such a big heart.

In between sessions at UTC, I had the opportunity to visit chaplaincies at both New South Wales University and Sydney University. Andrew Johnson and John Hirt are the Uniting Church of Australia's chaplains at these universities respectively. There is a daunting task, for they work in situations which are predominantly secular. Their presence created an oasis of hope. I was moved when I shared with the groups of students who were on fire sharing the Gospel to each other. It is not exaggerating to say that the Uniting Church of Australia is wise to keep on the candle lighting the corridors of higher learning institutions across the continent. I was to witness the results of the work of many University Chaplains across the nation when I later attended the School of Discipleship in Canberra. Scores of University Students attended a four-day workshop which was full of life and could not help but reflect on the work the Chaplains were doing.

Over the years, I have developed the acumen to preach on my personal experiences. To me, preaching starts at a personal level and I often take time to apply the word to my life before I emphasize on preaching to my audience. It is out of ignorance that one tries to deal with personal issues and rivalry from the pulpit. The gospel must prepare an individual for salvation and not just condemn them to hell. It must give people a new hope for salvation. While in Sydney, I preached to the West Epping Uniting Church congregation which was one of the biggest congregations that also includes several officers of the UnitingWorld, including its Chief Executive Officer Dr Kerry Enright.

I was also fortunate enough to visit the Opera House and the Sydney Harbour Bridge which are some of Australia's most treasured tourist attractions. The usual dull weather, that time of the year, suddenly changed to a bright day and I had this rare opportunity to sample the beautiful spots of this grand city. Sydney, by night, was a marvellous sight, especially for me who was coming from Harare where electricity comes in drips and droves. I could not help but thank God for such a wonderful opportunity to meet and to be invited for lunch by Sarah White, the founder of the Len Event, which has grown so big and works closely with the UnitingWorld in supporting various initiatives across Australia and the world.

Sydney-Home away from home

While I heartily salute my Australian host for a warm welcome and exquisite hosting during my stay, I was rather touched and exhilarated when I met two groups of Zimbabweans residing in Australia. Having the opportunity to meet your fellow countrymen in such a faraway place gave me a sense of home away from home. The union and memories shared were fulfilling. We all had our theories and understanding of the situation back home but what joined us together was the fact that we were all proud Zimbabweans with a shared vision for positive change in our motherland.

The first group particularly interested me in that they wanted me to preach to them, but they already had the scripture that they wanted me to preach from. When I arrived at their meeting place having chosen a text they instead gave me a passage to preach from, Matthew 13, which talks about the Parable of the Sower. The leader announced that he was inspired to choose that text for me. While this is not a very common arrangement, I didn't read much into this as I summoned heavenly wisdom and inspiration to guide me. I just prayed to God that He gives me the Word of impartation and that He ministers to the very needs of His people. It was a miracle to have the congregation thanking me for a God-given message and all I could do was glorify Him. Now I believe that God has given me the Word in season and, through it, revived His people and myself.

The second group was made up of members of the United Methodist Church. I, however noticed that most of these people were former members of the Methodist Church in Zimbabwe back home. While I have no problems with people fellowshipping in other congregation, if it is uplifting to their souls, I felt that my church, the Methodist Church in Zimbabwe, had an open challenge to continue shepherding its flock even when they leave for overseas.

I also discovered that these Zimbabweans who are largely economic refugees have very little time to rest and are having to cope with hard work as some have two jobs or more to do at the same time. This will be out of a desire to cushion themselves from financial woes.

I couldn't help but count Zimbabwe's losses as some of these people are qualified, experienced and dedicated that worked in various fields who are contributing to the success of another country's economy. Not to say that Australia or any other country that has opened up to these Zimbabwean economic refugees doesn't deserve this benefit. The Zimbabwean Government created this monster of brain drain through its failed policies and it must find ways of dealing with it. There is no need for blame shifting.

I salute the Australian Government for their Immigration Laws that allow for spouses to benefit once a partner is offered employment. Family members like in-laws and parents, can also visit for a period not exceeding three months and of those in employment, can actually be made Australian citizens after a period of three years.

Most of the Zimbabwean communities in Australia are very safe, with regards to family ties. Such rights are however a mere pipe dream back home where fellow Africans from such countries as Mozambique, Malawi and Zambia, to name but a few, are still considered as 'aliens', even after having spent decades in Zimbabwe and having positively contributed to the national cause. How do you label someone who has been a resident for 30 years, an alien? The thought of such complete disregard of people's God-given-rights irked me.

The United Theological College (UTC) also hosted me again and for a second time afforded me the treasured opportunity to tell the Zimbabwean story as it is. As I continued to interact with these brothers and sisters, I continued reflecting on our challenge as Zimbabweans, especially on the crying need for a lasting solution. At UTC, I was given a guest house, for my accommodation and would go for lunch and dinner at a member of the Faculty's houses for the duration I was there. I found this very humane and it made me not feel home-sick. I equally cherished my stay there and also the knowledge I gained from my interaction and presentations to the UTC family.

While I do not claim to be righteous, I could not help but revisit the piece of scripture that remarks that the steps of a righteous man are authored by God. It was very clear to me that my every step in Australia was indeed authored and guided by God. He was with me every step of the way.

The icing on the cake came when Clive invited me to be on the Editorial Committee of *Cross-Culture*, a Journal of Theology and Ministerial Practice. This journal is presently published by the United Theological College and it comes out twice a year. It is a peer review journal. Cross-Cultural-Theology is at the heart of the Journal, articles.

This is necessary because of the diaspora nature of our communities where individuals and groups of people have migrated at different times and find themselves interacting in new theological settings. This brings out a mosaic theological pattern that is understood through open discourses as covered in the Journal's series. I would be bringing the African flavour to the editorial committee. I intend to contribute articles, to this esteemed Journal, soon.

Adelaide

After having spent some quality and fulfilling time in Sydney, during the first week of July 2010 it was time to move on and my next port of call was Adelaide, where I was staying with Jim and Jan Rumery. I stayed for a whole month with the Rumerys. Jim and Jan 'discovered' me when they visited Zimbabwe in 2006. It was at the height of my struggle with the Government of Zimbabwe when together with concerned pastors, we had formed the Christian Alliance to spear head a campaign to help Zimbabweans come out of their crisis through non-violence means. We had just formed Christian Alliance at the end of 2005 after Operation *Murambatsvina*/Remove dirty when more that 700 000 people were left homeless after the government destroyed homes and business shelters for people who were trying to eke out a living.

Jim and Jan visited me when it was dangerous to do so because this was the time I was Bishop of the Harare West District of the Methodist Church in Zimbabwe. My office had been declared a 'no-go' area for the whites as my office was under 24-hour surveillance. Whenever I was visited by a white person, it was alleged that I was selling out the country to the white people, whatever that meant. The Rumerys were tourists and I had helped their white Zimbabwean friend who had lured them to come to Zimbabwe. I saw this man near my office, appearing lost and I offered to help. On his leaving, I gave him my business card and it was this card which made Jim and Jan want to see the man who had helped their friend. When they phoned, while on their way to the airport, they asked if they could visit me because they had enough time before their plane took off. We arranged to meet at my home albeit at their own risks, I told them. They did come, and friendship emerged instantly.

Four years later they arranged that I pay a visit to Australia. It was not an easy task, but Jim and Jan soldiered on until the trip was made possible. Such faith and hope are very rare to come by. These two never gave up like we did in Zimbabwe. Together with the Adelaide Pilgrim Uniting Church and Northern Illawara Uniting Church they pledged to make my trip a success through putting their resources together. Jim and Jan were then members of Northern Illawara Uniting Church for which Jim was the Missionary Secretary. Jim sold the idea of linking what I was doing with the Church in Bulli. A mutual relationship was created which has seen us walking together and as they prayed for our situation, in Zimbabwe. They got first-hand information about the plight of the people, some of whom had lost limb and life. Now Jim and Jan for the last 22 months are residents of Adelaide which bought the idea of sponsoring my trip to Australia even if no one knew me except for the word of the Rumerys. Such is the trust that only comes from an open society.

On my second day in Adelaide, I was given the privilege to be at a Reflection Centre Nunyara, where I spent a whole day on my own, reflecting on my life and getting perspective. It is a thing called for especially where durable peace and stability prevails to spend some reflection time on your won. It somehow refreshes your mind and allows you to reflect on your past and plan.

Unfortunately, this is a dream for Zimbabweans who must worry about their next meal and next dollar every minute of the day. The most painful reality is that all this worrying and trouble is not a natural development but a clear result of human greed and insensitiveness.

It was at the Reflection Centre that I met Matt Cornu, who had also come for the same experience. Matt is a Uniting Church minister responsible for Rural Ministry in South Australia. He had also come to a quiet time and the conversations we had led to the Riverland and Murray Mallee familiarization trip which I embarked on some fifteen days later with him. I have also had some rural ministry experience with my church in Zimbabwe and this has given me a better understanding of all the dynamics of such a ministry. I have also developed better appreciation of working with rural folks and of understanding their needs. Being offered an opportunity to visit rural ministry, even in Australia, was thus pulsating.

Rejuvenated and reinvigorated after the Reflection Centre interval, I then headed to the Uniting College of Leadership and Theology where I had the opportunity to lecture to Aboriginal students and other ministerial students. I am sure many people the world over knows about the history of the Aborigine people in Australia, the challenges they have endured and the pain that they have undergone. Sharing with such people and especially coming from Zimbabwe where the government of the day has reduced the ordinary people to beggars in their motherland was indeed a gratifying undertaking. You would realise gentle reader that the pain that the Aborigine people have endured over decades is very much akin to the suffering that the ordinary Zimbabweans have had to content with, from the colonial era to the post-independence era in which the former liberator has fast become the oppressor.

After the lectures to the Aborigine students and Ministerial students, I also managed to speak to the Synod for South Australia which has Adelaide as its Capital. Those with prior knowledge of how main line churches like the Methodist Church operate would understand the importance of a Synod in as far as strengthening ministerial work is concerned. It is a very important meeting where key decision on the way forward with mission work are made and necessary changes, ideology and leadership are made but all in a very democratic and consultative manner.

The Synod had a session on 'Fresh Expressions,' a new way of expressing people's faith outside the normal church structures which started in the United Kingdom. A UK based cleric led the sessions and a lot of debate ensued. We learnt from each other as we reflected on the matter. What I heard as new developments and as having started in the UK have actually been and still are everyday phenomena in Africa. The so-called 'established' or 'historical' churches are now far outnumbered by 'new expressions,' which are the emerging congregations which are growing so big across the continent of Africa. While Australia can learn from the UK, it can also turn its eyes closer to Africa to learn how churches are emerging and growing every day in Africa.

After the South Australian Synod, I also had the opportunity to preach to specific congregations in that community. I had an opportunity to preach to the largest congregation of Sudanese people based in Adelaide, of over 300 members. This congregation is based at Mahaun Uniting Church.

My sermons touched many souls and in all this, I didn't forget to call for the prayers and support of these fellow brothers and sisters, both of other African nations and for my native-Zimbabwe. I also preached to nationals of Liberia and Sierra Leone who are shepherded by local Uniting Church congregations. I believe in the power of prayer to change things and in as much as I am a pragmatist, I still feel that change borders on God's intervention.

I also addressed pertinent issues like *'Conflict in Society – the Role of the Church' and Politics and Power Struggles – What a price justice.'* All these sessions which were held at Pilgrim Uniting Church, plus one at Synod, were ably moderated by Marelle Harisun. She is also a member of the Christian Council of Australia.

Pilgrim Uniting Church Guest Preacher

I was also a Guest Preacher at the Pilgrim Uniting Church, where that month of July, I would preach two to three times a Sunday and give speeches and lectures during the week. The organisers of these services, lectures and speech presentations did well to advertise them and often, I would speak to a very encouraging audience. I also made many friends while speaking at the Synod. Pilgrim Church is special in the sense that it underwrote my trip to Australia. The leadership of Tony Eldridge Sandy Boyce and their faith in engaging someone they had never had seen before to be a Guest Preacher for the whole month at their Church was a challenge to me. Such faith and trust are rare to come by these days, especially when you are coming from a different culture and background.

While in Adelaide, I also had time to visit Jennie Hackett's farm. Jennie is a member of Pilgrim Uniting Church. I spent a whole day feeding cattle at the farm. Being the farmer that I am back home, I could not help but be happy. For a moment, it felt like I was back at my farm in Zimbabwe. Feeding the cattle at a farm just outside Adelaide and gelling with the smell of the cow dung gave me a great feeling and creeping nostalgia.

After the farm experience I also had an appointment with the Moderator of the South Australian Synod, the Rev. Rod Dyson and his officers for more that two hours. We also had an opportunity to exchange notes on the mission work after which I had another chance for sightseeing, I certainly couldn't ask for more. Without knowing it another week was over.

I also met a lot on Zimbabweans who had heard of my visit on the radio and through other local advertising channels. Forward in Faith Ministries, better known as Zimbabwe Assembles of God in Africa (ZAOGA) in native Zimbabwe also hosted me and gave me an opportunity to preach to their congregation. I was also invited by the United Methodist Church (UMC) in Australia and out of that congregation 12 were Methodist Church in Zimbabwe members who had joined the UMC because they had no close alternative in Australia.

One of the days I did present a public lecture at Flinders University. This was organised through the help of Rev Geoff Boyce the Uniting Church Chaplain at the University. I spoke of the '*Church and Political Change in Zimbabwe.'* I shared with the group the struggle of a divided church. Where one section of the church tries to play it safe with the government by not raising pertinent issues. Those who decided to speak on behalf of the people were victimised. I was personally victim who both by the Government and my own Church. It was only after the formation of the Government of National Unity that my church admitted me back to full appointment. When the situation was tough my church asked me to part ways with it. For two years I was doing my own thing. Now I am back because there is peace. What an irony! Is it not the role of the church to struggle with the oppressed? I wonder.

Encounter with Indigenous Leaders and my message to them and to the world

My first encounter with the indigenous leaders was at the Uniting College for Leadership and Theology in Adelaide. It did not take time before we were sharing similar stories. Richard Wallace introduced me to his group which shared with my experience as an African from a country that was once colonised. I also met the Congress, -Uniting Aboriginal and Islander Christian Congress. I shared with them my story of hate for Mugabe which had deteriorated to the point of me switching off the television each time he appeared on television. I had been arrested five times without any charge. This was done just to break my resolve. For some time, I tried to defend my position until one day I just decided to forgive him. After I had done that, I felt relieved. I felt the burden I was carrying lifted. I felt like growing wings. The scripture that says, *"Come to me all who labour and are heavy laden, and I will give you rest. Take my yoke upon you and learn from me; for I am gentle and lowly in heart, and you will find rest for your souls. For my yoke is easy and my burden in light."* (Matthew 11 vs 28ff) became very vivid to me.

Aboriginal people, like my people back home, are in the danger of carrying heavy burdens of unforgiving for the rest of their lives. The greatest danger is to pass on that hatred to the next generation. The time we fail to forgive, we load it upon ourselves and we only do great disservice to ourselves. Those whom we say wronged us may not even be thinking about it or troubling themselves about it. It is true, however, that they do carry guilty in their lives but sometimes they do not realize it. It is only when the guilt and the hurting people open to each other that true reconciliation is achieved. Kevin Rudd the Australian prime minister did well a few years ago to ask for forgiveness but a lot must be done to make the faith step produce results.

Since I arrived in Australia many people there expected me to bring a message of hatred for President Mugabe but were disappointed because I showed a spirit of forgiveness. This is shown in my addresses when I shared my story of forgiveness. In several instances some individuals would bolt out of the session, lamenting that all along they had been praying for Mugabe to die.

I told them the story of Pharaoh the Great African Leader who enslaved the Israelites for over 400 years.

When God sent Moses to liberate the Israelites God at one-time hardened Pharaoh's heart. I am sure every Israelite would have wished Pharaoh dead, but God did not answer that prayer.

Several Zimbabweans would have wished Mugabe dead, but God did not respond positively to such a prayer. Instead, He hardened Mugabe's heart. God does that for a purpose. If Pharaoh was not as wicked, perhaps the Church Fathers would have found it very difficult to include the story of the bondage of Israel in the Old Testament. Likewise, God was hardening Mugabe's heart for a purpose, who knows?

A few weeks before I came to Australia I had an opportunity to attend the then Zimbabwean Prime Minister's, Morgan Tsvangirai's, wife's memorial service at Malbereign Methodist Church in Harare. I was late for the service and so when arrived, the service, was already on. My wife and I were ushered into the Church right in front where there was some space, left for the church was full. And whom did I seat close to? Mugabe sat just a splitting distance between me and him. Had this happened before I had not forgiven him, I could have turned down the offer of the seat in front. But because it came when I had forgiven him, I was so happy to be close to the man I had forgiven a couple of months earlier. When he was asked to speak to the congregation, I could not help but marvel at the youthfulness of Mugabe. He had just celebrated is 86 birthdays then! But looking at him he was just like 56 years old.

Therefore, people may pray for someone to die but God may reward the person with good health. And all this is done for a purpose. It is not for us to wish anyone dead. What we can only do best is to forgive, and we are the winners in the end. I am not in any way saying that we should condone the bad things our leaders do. The law must take its own course for justice to prevail. Let no one harbour ill for anyone. Let not the sun go down before you have forgiven the one who has wronged you as the Scriptures say. When we are angry and unforgiving we are open to be used even by any force. We tend to drink too much alcohol because we are depressed by something which we have not corrected. We turn to drugs because we are hurting. We turn to crime because we are not at peace with ourselves.

The Aborigines of Australia, like the Africans, may defend their position of always hurting because of what has happened to them in the past. This must come to an end if they are to progress. I am not in any way saying that we should pretend that all is well, no, instead we should be open to each other and I demand that we confess to each other.

The cross that we carry is we want to live together while we have forgiven each other for the past wrongs, we do not have to forget though. Forgetting is not a virtue. Even Christ did not command us to forget the events that lead to the cross. Instead he commanded us to remember when he said at the Last Supper, "Do this in remembrance of me." Since the death of Christ on the cross we remember the event like it happened recently.

Living a victorious life means to live with people who have wronged you and you have forgiven them. This is my message to all the peoples of this world who have been wronged and to those who have also wronged others. We may not have been involved personally but our ancestors may have done it on our behalf. We cannot run away from the actions of our ancestors. If we do not correct them now, they will haunt us and the future generations until they try to make peace with each other. As we read this, let us commit ourselves to working for true peace that comes through opening to each other and deal with the past squarely.

The message above was taken heartily by my audience. We promised to share the message across to everyone who was prepared to listen to our story. Our wish was if we could have more opportunities to share such a deep understanding of life. I promised, in faith, that I was going to come back with my dear wife, Asiusinaye, and share more insights about forgiving and living a victorious life both as Australians and Africans. This must begin somewhere, and I was convinced that it would catch on across the continent of Australia and the world over.

The words of the NSW Congress Chairperson, Dianne Torrens, were very instructive, *"As an Indigenous leader I often tell my people that progress will come, to draw on your faith in God and believe that you can do it. When you find yourself broken, in a ditch and with no strength, you need God's faith to know that He will turn the situation around."* (From *'Message Stick'* the magazine of the Uniting Aboriginal and Islander Christian Congress, Autumn/2010 pg. 9). From the same source one lady an Indigenous Ministry and Theology student demonstrates that change is possible change. When she says, *"I was hooked on alcohol for two years. The addiction was killing me, my kids and my family and even though I knew I was often drunk I would call out to the Lord for help to get me out of the situation. Alcohol had a real stronghold on me. Initially it was fun but it soon took control of my life but that was until the Lord turned my life around."* pg. 15.

Riverland and Murray Mallee Tour

The journey took us to Bermera, Walkerie, Berri where we put up for the night, Pinnaroo and Lameroo and there are Uniting Church congregations. Matt Cornu, who took me there, had been their minister, coming from Adelaide. At each place, we had reflection meetings. We discussed the problems that these congregations faced because of the absence of the Resident Minister. My experience from the Institute of Theological Reflections Today helped me to bring out relevant issues affecting these congregations.

They agreed that they were lacking pastoral care from a minister. They also needed constant supervision. New members did not trust them. Some prospective members left before they settled because they were expecting the presence of a minister and but the advantages they picked on were that they were now caring for each other like they never did before. They had the freedom to do those things they had always wanted to do but could not do because of the minister. This made them a very close-knit family a thing which they could not do when they were cushioned by the constant presence of the minister. They learnt to conduct funerals and to give Communion. They saved money because they did not have a minister to pay. They could use the funds they had for caring for those in need. By the end of the trip we had clocked just over 900km. At least I had an opportunity to sees Australia's back pack.

Before I left Pilgrim Church, I was invited to a farewell party where I was given a gift, including an album with most of the photos I took, and I was taken during my stay in Australia. It was indeed a pleasant surprise which I will cherish for a very long time. May the good Lord continue to bless the people of Adelaide Pilgrim Church.

Canberra

I stayed in Canberra for a period of seven days. The first three days I stayed with Richardson's family. While Canberra had its fare share of experiences for me with regards to my ministry and humanitarian work, I also enjoyed the sights of the Parliament and the Embassy for the Aboriginal people, a protest embassy which is in the form of a tent built in front of the Parliament. That the Aboriginal people's embassy is built in front of Parliament and is in form of a tent appears to stem from their dismay at the disregard of their rights and their painful experiences in the past. That, for me, is an indication of a people in a desperate need of healing and healing of memories as is the case in Zimbabwe. It appears the Aborigines still harbour so much hurt and pain and a lot needs to be done for their healing.

I also liked the Canberra tour that I had with Dan and Maureen Etherington and the coffee and conversation that I had at the Kippax Uniting Church under the theme, "The Church's role in the future of Zimbabwe." Dan hosted the meeting. I also had the opportunity of meeting Pam Pelling, again once missionary to Zimbabwe several years ago. She was 90. She became my English mentor when we stayed together in Harare. She had heard of my visit and surprised me by coming to the meeting.

While politicians have developed a knack of side-lining churches and sometimes threatening them whenever they have a say in national issues, the fact is that Christians have a role to play. The Uniting Church in Australia's *Statement on the Human Rights* highlights that human beings are created in the image of God who is three persons in open, joyful interaction. The Uniting Church thus believes that every person is precious and entitled to live with dignity because they are God's children, and that each person's life and rights needs to be protected or the human community (and its reflection of God) and all people are dismissed. They have some encouraging contributions to the national human rights discourse.

The Uniting Church believes that in Jesus Christ we discern that which is truly human, and that Christians are called to love their neighbours as they love themselves and extend that love to their enemies. It is therefore the love of God in Christ Jesus which motivates us to live out this calling by working for peace with justice in our church, our communities and the world. The recognition of human rights for the Uniting Church is an affirmation of the dignity of all people and essential for achieving peace with justice. Our leaders must see Christ in every person by doing so, they won't go wrong. Egotism is exactly what is ruining service to humanity as leaders care more about self-enrichment than satisfying the needs of those they lead.

After having enjoyed the Canberra sights, I was afforded the opportunity to meet the Uniting Care team, which is a service arm of the Church that deals with issues like justice and health needs of the people among others. Just the realisation that the Uniting Church has a high regard for the rights of the people gave me better inspiration to continue fighting for justice in Zimbabwe. For Zimbabweans however, a lot more needs to be done because the situation at hand goes in tune with the old age reality that rights should not be asked for but are demanded for. They are not freely given but are taken. We must fight against more ruthless forces in the form of a government that has far outlived its time span and is only ruling by force and coercion.

At the Uniting Care, I also had lunch with the outgoing Director, Lin Hatfield Dodd's, who was also vying for Senatorship. It was encouraging for me to have a Christian leader vying for a national post as compared to the Zimbabwean situation where we have Christians being asked to stay away from politics. When politics is simply the art and science of governance, our daily experiences affect every citizen. I believe that not having some Christian influence in government would do the nation of Zimbabwe more harm than good. The few Christians that dabble in politics or maybe the politicians that dabble in Christianity do it out of opportunism in a bid to get the Christian vote especially given that Christians form more that 80% of the Zimbabwean population.

In Canberra, I had the chance to relate with Rev Dr James Haire, from the Centre for Christianity and Culture. The name 'Centre for Christianity and Culture' somehow took me aback. Lest some argue that our advocacy for democratic space in Zimbabwe is informed by the white man's Christian faith, a closer look at the Zimbabwean culture clearly reflects that respect for humanity and people's rights has always been a demand that every form of leadership has had to respect. Whichever way you look at it, respect for the people's human and God given rights is a necessary reality. It befuddles the mind why our current crop of leadership has chosen to ignore people's rights. They are so preoccupied with power retention that they have very little, if any, regard for people's rights.

School of Discipleship

During my last 4 days in Canberra, I went to the School of Discipleship at Greenhills with the university students from across Australia, where they had conference and crusade. The School ran from the 9th to the 12th of July 2010 and I shared a room with Doug Hewitt and I also had the opportunity to speak about my experiences back home and most of these meetings were oversubscribed. I also had the rare opportunity to meet and share briefly with the Uniting Church President, the Rev Alistair Macrae who also visited the School of Discipleship. Just to give you a run through of the School of Discipleship's perception of me and the work that I have been doing with the Christian Alliance, I have decided to reproduce a profile that they published in the special event's publication under electives that made presentations from various corners of the world. Below is the excerpt as produced in the programme publications.

Storytelling of faith from Zimbabwe: Bishop Kadenge

In 2005 a group of like minded clergy and lay people from various denominations in Zimbabwe formed Christian Alliance. It came into

185

being because of the extraordinarily difficult social and political situation in their country. They felt the Christian community was very quiet while the ordinary people's democratic space was shrinking by the day. Christian Alliance offered to speak on behalf of the silent majority against the social ills of the time and Bishop Kadenge was chosen as its Convenor. In mid-2009, he resumed full ministry in the church as a lecturer at the theological college. He was invited to pioneer a subject Religion and Current Social Issues (RCSI), to share his experiences with Christian Alliance, and the imperative for the church to engage with contemporary issues.

This elective is an opportunity to hear some of Bishop Kadenge's reflections on his experience.

Bishop Kadenge joined ministry in 1978, undertaking theological study in his home country of Zimbabwe as well as in South Africa and the UK. He completed his doctorate on 1998. Ministry placements have included rural congregations in Zimbabwe and chaplain in Methodist High Schools. He lectured at the United Theological College for seven years, also serving as chaplain and Vice Principal during that time.

Bishop Kadenge is widely travelled and is involved in leadership in many organisations including the Southern African Federation of the disabled, Zimbabwe Advocacy office based in Geneva and Zimbabwe Ecumenical network based in Brussels. He is the founder and Director of the Institute of Theological Reflection Today.

It is my sincere hope that my experiences and the interaction that I had at the School of Discipleship will help inspire fellow Christian leaders to desist from preaching the gospel of the cross without looking at the practical realities facing their member. Ministry certainly calls for more than just preaching. I believe that the whole undertaking somehow strengthened the Zimbabwean Christian and indeed national community with Australia and more positive interaction and partnerships will come out of it. I am convinced that Australia now understands the Zimbabwean crisis from a Christian leader's perspective as compared to that of a politician.

A take on Diplomacy

The world has become a global village and diplomatic relations has taken a centre stage in the way nations relate. It is equally true that President Mugabe's grand standing and diplomatic blunders during the height of our economic decline has led Zimbabwe to become more of a pariah state. It was thus after the successful School of Disciples experience that I then took time to visit the Zimbabwean Embassy in Australia in Canberra.

I just felt enthralled by the idea of better understanding how the embassy operates and the roles they are playing towards nation building. The Zimbabwean ambassador was very happy to see me and had time to give me a tour of the place and introduce me to her team at the same time allowing me to share my beliefs and vision for the great nation that we share, Zimbabwe.

No one person can claim to be more Zimbabwean than the other and we have all contributed positively in our small ways to nation building. It is only suicidal for one to continue holding on to power regardless of the realities on the ground simply because they feel they had some positive contributions in the past. Even cup winning football coaches get fired when the results are no longer coming. In one of the mother languages in Zimbabwe; Shona we say *"matakadya kare haanyaradzi mwana"* meaning you cannot comfort a hungry and crying child by retelling stories of how you once fed her well in the past. You need to deal with her present state of hunger if you are to win her affection. Our leaders must awaken to this reality.

Service to Humanity

My pilgrim to Australia also gave me better insights on what leadership and people centred services is all about. The School of Discipleship in Australia asserts that if we idolise wealth we create poverty, if we idolise success, we create the less fortunate; if we idolise power, we create powerlessness; If we idolise anger and hate, we devalue healing and transformation; if we idolise violence, we devalue life; if we live non-violently, we herald God's peaceable reign; if we live as radical disciples, we subvert the dominion paradigm and if we live for what Jesus lives for, we resist the paralysing official consensus and we change the world.

Ours is to make an informed choice and make sure that we leave a legacy that we are going to be proud of even when we lie in our graves. Who said durable peace and national cohesion, meaningful progress, born out of the dignity in humanity is pipedream? My personal experiences in the fight for democracy in Zimbabwe have shown that it is never too late to make amends. Our political need to respect the human dignity of its people and see to it that they throw away the pretence and selflessness for servitude and empathy.

Our political leaders simply need to awaken to the reality that leadership is more about service to the people than useless grandstanding and giving some useless speeches about sovereignty and how they liberated the country. Yes, they liberated the country and then what? While we all celebrate independence in Zimbabwe, the present reality is, there is, no democratic space in Zimbabwe and people are hungry and hurting lot. The people's human dignity has been eroded to say the least.

When human dignity or a people's rights are tempered with, either by way of deliberate power retention or machinations especially in undemocratic nations or in cases of unplanned conflict there is need for redress as a complete disregard of that anomaly is a sure recipe for disaster. A disregard of that sense of human dignity and stability disturbs world order hence the need for programs, like national healing and healing of memories in conflict areas. Closer home, countries like Ruwanda, Uganda and South Africa to name a few have successfully carried out these corrective interventions. Such noble realisations have in some instances helped to entrench durable peace. The same is now happening in our country and every self-respecting Zimbabwean, the principals included must see the opportunities and we hope that national healing can bring to our nation.

One Barbra Deutschman, an Australian Christian author writes that when someone has hurt or slighted us, we feel a natural sense of indignation. We know that they have violated our sense of who we are. This response is consistent with our natural knowledge of ourselves as people made in the image of God, worthy of dignity and respect. It is equally true that we all have individual egos and pride and any disregard of our beliefs and values even minus a violent unleashing of terror is hurting. The unfortunate thing under such circumstance is that not many perpetrators of hurt and violence are ready to say sorry or make the slightest attempt at correcting their wrongs. This has catastrophic results and implications in world affairs and the sooner we wake up to that the better.

BIBLIOGRAPHY

1. Aina Tade, Akina, and Moyo, Bhekinkosi, ED. <u>Giving to Help, and Helping to Give,</u> Amallion, Trust Africa, 2013

2. Arnold W. E, <u>Here to Stay</u>, The Book Guild Limited, 1985

3. Bakare, Sebastian, <u>My Right to Land,</u> Delsink Publishers, 1993

4. Bosch, David, <u>Witness to the World,</u> Marshall, Morgan & Scott- London, 1980

5. Bucher, Hubert, <u>Spirits and Power</u>, (An Analysis of Shona Cosmology), Oxford University Press, 1980

6. Chikuku, Tendai, ED., <u>Media for Peace</u>, EDICISA, 2005

7. Chitando, Ezra, and Hadebe, Nontando, Ed., <u>Compassionate Circles,</u> EHAIA Series, 2009

8. Choto, Nathan F., <u>African and Western Missionary Partnership in Christian Mission; Rhodesia- Zimbabwe 1897-1968</u>, Morris Publishing, 2006

9. Dodge, Ralphe E, <u>The Unpopular Missionary,</u> Fleming H Revell Company, 1960

10. Frazier, Allie M, <u>Issues in Religion</u>, D. Van Nostrand Company, 1975

11. Kaulemu, David, <u>Political Participation in Zimbabwe,</u> Miserior AFCAST, 2010

12. Kurewa, John Wesley Zvamunondiita, <u>African Pastors-Teachers,</u> Discipliship Resources, 2011

13. Minnie, Jeanette, ED. <u>Outside the Ballot Box,</u> 2005/6

14. Musa, David, <u>African-American African</u> (A Confluent of African Traditional Religion) Authorhouse, 2015

15. Muzorewa, Gwinyai Henry, <u>An African Theology of Mission.</u> Edwin Press, 1990

16. Niebuhr, H. Richard, <u>Christ and Culture,</u> Harper & Row, Publishers, 1951

17. Nyanjaya, Ananias K., <u>Female Grief,</u> Connexional Bookshop, 2017

18. Obama, Barack, <u>The Audacity of Hope</u>, Canongate, 2007

19. Samkange, S., <u>On trail for my Country</u>, London, 1967

20. Spong, John Selby, <u>Born of a Woman,</u> Harper San Francisco, 1971

21. Vicencio, Charles Villa, <u>Between Christ and Caesar</u>, William B. Eerdmans Publishing Company, 1986

22. _____, <u>The Truth will make you Free,</u> Churches in Manicaland, 2006

23. Zvobgo, C.J.M., <u>The Wesleyan Methodist Missions in Zimbabwe 1891-1945,</u> University of Zimbabwe Publications, Harare, 1991

Printed in the United States
By Bookmasters